LETS GO United States of America!

Jobs! Jobs! Jobs!

The Donald J. Trump Way!

Where Did The Jobs Go?
How Can We Get Them Back?

If you are out hunting for a job, you better be carrying a scattergun because jobs are plain and simple hard to find and hard to get in the sights. I know you won't be using a Purdey "shotgun," which is the best, even if you are job hunting. That's because, if you are unemployed and you have $100,000 to spend on a house or a gun, I'll bet that you would take living indoors over having the best job hunting shotgun in the marketplace. Too bad it were not that easy. Donald Trump knows how to solve everybody's job problem.

Jobs are hard to come by and you can blame the government for that. In twelve essays, we discuss Jobs! Jobs! Jobs!. We'll tell you where they have gone and how to bring those rascals back. And, folks, we plan to bring those Jobs back alive. Donald Trump is our man to get the job of jobs done! He is the only presidential candidate ever who hired a person for a job! Wow!

AF814012

LETS GO PUBLISH

BRIAN W. KELLY

 Editor, Melissa L. Sabol
Jobs! Jobs! Jobs! The Donald J. Trump Solution! Author Brian W. Kelly
Where Did They Go? How Can We Get Them Back?

Referenced Material : *The information in this book has been obtained through personal and third party observations, interviews, and copious research. Where unique information has been provided or extracted from other sources, those sources are acknowledged within the text of the book itself or at the end of the chapter in the Sources Section. Thus, there are no formal footnotes nor is there a bibliography section. Any picture that does not have a source was taken from various sites on the Internet with no credit attached. If resource owners would like credit in the next printing, please email publisher.*

Published by: ....LETS GO PUBLISH!
Publisher: ....Brian P. Kelly
Editor: ....Melissa L. Sabol
Mail Location: .... P.O. Box 834, Scranton, PA
Web site ....www.letsgopublish.com

Library of Congress Copyright Information Pending
Book Cover Design by Michele Thomas, Editing by Melissa L. Sabol

ISBN Information: The International Standard Book Number (ISBN) is a unique machine-readable identification number, which marks any book unmistakably. The ISBN is the clear standard in the book industry. 159 countries and territories are officially ISBN members. The Official ISBN For this book is on the outside cover: **978-0-9980848-0-0**

The price for this work is : **$12.95 USD**

10 9 8 7 6 5 4 3 2 1

Release Date: May 2010; September 2016

LETS GO PUBLISH!

Dedication

I dedicate this book

*to all of the wonderful Americans out there,
struggling to get by at a time in our Country's history which
is very uncertain.*

*I hope the job that you have, you can keep,
and that if you are temporarily unemployed, I hope that
your next job is your best ever.*

*Please take nothing for granted as I regret to say that our
government may very well not be on your side in whatever it
is you choose to do next.*

*Be wary, be smart, and make sure that
everybody you choose to trust in the coming years
is trustworthy.*

I wish you all the best.

Acknowledgments

I would like to thank many people for helping me in this effort.

I appreciate all the help that I have received in putting this book together as well as all of my other 78 published books.

My printed acknowledgments had become so large that book readers "complained" about going through too many pages to get to page one of the text.

And, so to permit me more flexibility, I put my acknowledgment list online, and it continues to grow. Believe it or not, it once cost about a dollar more to print each book.

Thank you and God bless you all for your help.

Please check out www.letsgopublish.com to read the latest version of my heartfelt acknowledgments updated for this book. Click the bottom of the Main menu!

Thank you all!

Table of Contents

BTW, not telling the full truth is also a lie.

The Washington Examiner was demything the Obama jobs claims and they have a ton of them on their site. This little update from 12/1/09 is about how most of them look:

"Roughly 2,000 new imaginary stimulus jobs have been added to the map, including hundreds of reported Head Start jobs that were actually just pay raises." Maybe it was just a fib?

Robert Reich is a former Labor Secretary under Clinton. He is now a Professor at UC Berkeley. He knows his stuff but occasionally from my perspective has too much cool-aid brewed from the hard left. Reich actually believes the stuff so he is not a liar. He tries to give the hard left stuff a good spin every chance he can.

He was clearly laboring in a recent article to find something good to say to college seniors about to come out into the business world. The best he could do was that they would probably get jobs but not as good and not with as much promise as days gone by. And, don't expect big pay raises, Reich knows his stuff:

"Since the start of the Great Recession in December 2007, the U.S. economy has shed 8.4 million jobs and failed to create another 2.7 million required by an ever-larger pool of potential workers .... The Great Recession has accelerated a structural shift in the economy that had been slowly building for years. Companies have used the downturn to aggressively trim payrolls, making cuts they've been reluctant to make before. Outsourcing abroad has increased dramatically. Companies have discovered that new software and computer technologies have made many workers in Asia and Latin America almost as productive as Americans, and that the Internet allows far more work to be efficiently moved to another country without loss of control."

Thank you Mr. Professor, Mr Secretary Reich. Mr. Reich is not a liar.

Jack Cafferty seems to hate conservatives. He, like Mr. Reich does not seem to like the "l" word. Nobody expected Jack Cafferty to be throwing his best shots at Obama on any message but like many liberals who are not on the very hard left, Cafferty is not interested in lying and he is not interested in carrying the water for a liar. Many were very surprised at Cafferty's excoriation of Barack Hussein Obama and the most inept Congress God has ever permitted to be assembled.

"White House and Democratic leaders will hold informal, that's another word for secret negotiations, meant to shut Republicans and the public out of the process. That's a far cry from the election, when then candidate Obama pledged to "broadcast the negotiations on C-Span so that the American people can see what the choices are."
...
"President Obama hasn't even made a token effort to keep his campaign promises of more openness and transparency in government. It was all just another lie that was told to get elected."

Thank you for the truth, Mr. Cafferty

Now,here are a few more notes and quotes about lies and liars. Most of the ones coming up are light but this Preface will end with a very heavy thought.

"Lies are powerful instruments of deception, and the better the liar, the more powerful the instrument."
Brian Kelly -- yep, that's me

"Liars share with those they deceive the desire not to be deceived."
Sissela Bok

"Men are liars. We'll lie about lying if we have to. I'm an algebra liar. I figure two good lies make a positive."
Tim Allen

"All governments are run by liars and nothing they say should be believed."
I. F. Stone

"All pitchers are liars or crybabies."
Yogi Berra

"Anyone who claims to be good at lying is obviously bad at lying. Thus - as a writer myself - I cannot comment on whether or not writers are exceptionally good liars, because whatever I said would actually mean its complete opposite."
Chuck Klosterman

"The men the American people admire most extravagantly are the most daring liars; the men they detest most violently are those who try to tell them the truth."
Henry Louis Mencken

Ladies and Gentleman, I regret that the poking of fun is over.

This next note on lying is from the Minister of Propaganda from the Reich (that's not Reisch). This quote is so spooky, it gives me the creeps.

While you are reading this, ask yourself if a man who was trying to weasel out of saying that his vote in the Illinois Senate to permit infanticide (killing aborted babies because they were not supposed to live) was based on the fact that the child [may not really be a person right after birth] or [if the out-of-womb surviving child is not a viable person] " is worth any of your time. Because he is the President, we have no choice of course. How would Barack Hussein Obama feel about this quote? Perhaps it already is part of his socialist mantra, and that is the spookiest thought of all.

"If you tell a lie big enough and keep repeating it, people will eventually come to believe it. The lie can be maintained only for such time as the State can shield the people from the political, economic and/or military consequences of the lie. It

Donald Trump Addresses American Legion Convention in Cincinnati, September 1, 2016

Before we move on the text of the Trump speech. I would like to introduce the Donald Trump American Legion Speech that I listened closely to today. Hopefully you will read it word for word below.

As a proud member of the American Legion, Post 815, in Wilkes-Barre Township, I admit that I was a bit jealous of the wonderful men and women in Cincinnati attending the National Convention on September 1, 2016. I interrupted my work day to take the pleasure of watching the entire Donald Trump Speech at 9:00 AM.

Donald Trump is an amazing man and he is about to be a great American hero right after he is sworn in on Inauguration Day, Friday, Jan. 20, 2017 to become the 45th President of the United States of America.

He made this great speech in Cincinnati. It was just hours after he delivered a groundbreaking speech on immigration Wednesday night in Arizona. Trump had to be exhausted but he looked fresh as a daisy addressing the veterans who have given so much to the country. He flew overnight to the Queen City Thursday to address veterans at the American Legion National Convention.

The speech as you will soon know by reading the text below was outstanding. You can hear and see the entire speech if you would like on the Internet. Mr. Trump was impeccable in his delivery.

While watching the speech, I recognized how it tied many of Mr. Trump's policies together and of course jobs was a very important part of the speech. That is why I selected this entire speech as the opening chapter for this book on Jobs! Jobs! Jobs! The Trump Way! I had just finished editing the final essay in this book last night. Nonetheless, I quickly made the change to include the Trump speech that he delivered so eloquently to our American Legion Veterans today.

A Succinct and pithy patriotic presentation

This presentation by Donald Trump was made with a number of interruptions for applause made by our nation's veterans who are long-time members of the American Legion. It made me proud to be a Legionnaire. The veterans were enjoying their annual national convention and had the pleasure of hearing our next president on the last day of their convention. It was a wonderful presentation and it kicks off this book Jobs! Jobs! Jobs! in the perfect way. Please enjoy!

Editor's note: The following is the full transcript of prepared remarks from* Donald Trump *at the American Legion convention in Cincinnati, Ohio, as released by the Trump campaign:

Thank you all so much. What an honor and a privilege to speak today to the American Legion.

I thank Commander Dale Barnett, your vice commanders, and your constitutional officers. You have all done such an incredible job.

The men and women of the American Legion represent the best of America. Strength, courage, selfless devotion. Your organization, and its members, have done so much to defend our country, our flag, and to advance the cause of Americanism – not Globalism.

We are in your debt.

I will never let you down.

Together, we are going to work on so many shared goals. But I want to begin by discussing one goal that I know is so important to all of you: promoting American pride and patriotism in America's schools.

In A Trump Administration, I plan to work directly with the American Legion to uphold our common values and to help ensure they are taught to America's children. We want our kids to learn the incredible achievements of America's history, its institutions, and its heroes.

We agreed in the meeting on the need to stop the illegal flow of guns, drugs, cash and people across the border and to take out the cartels.

We also talked about the importance of working to keep jobs and wealth in our hemisphere. A more prosperous Mexico means fewer illegal border crossings, and a better market for products made in the United States.

When I am President, I am going to look at every trade deal we have across the world and see what steps must be taken to protect American jobs and create new opportunities for American workers. We will fight for every last American job.

We're going to show ourselves and the world again what a strong and growing American economy looks like.

We are going to give major tax relief to every worker and small business in this country, bring thousands of new companies and millions of new jobs back to our shores – and unleash an American Energy Revolution.

We will also be appointing justices who will defend our Constitution.

I will nominate men and women to the court who meet the high standard of Antonin Scalia, judges who have the wisdom and integrity to follow the law and not just make it up.

Above all, these next four years, I will be uncompromising in the defense of the United States and our friends and allies. We are going to end the era of nation-building, and create a new foreign policy – joined by our partners in the Middle East – that is focused on destroying ISIS and Radical Islamic Terrorism. We will extend the hand of friendship to any nation that will work with us in good faith on this vital mission.

At the same time, we will change our immigration screening procedures to help keep terrorists and extremists out of our country. That includes stopping the influx of Syrian refugees. My opponent wants a 550% increase. I, on the other hand, want to build a safe zone overseas – and use the money saved to invest in America.

It is time to create a New American Future – for you, your children, and all American children yet to come.

In this future, we will have an honest government – and that includes an honest State Department, not Pay-For-Play. Government access and favors will no longer be for sale, and important email records will no longer be deleted and digitally bleached.

We will also have an efficient and responsible federal budget – no more waste, no more throwing away taxpayer dollars.

Once more, we will have a government of, by and for the people.

It will be an inclusive society, one that offers hope and opportunity to every part of this country – including our inner cities. We will ensure that every child in this land, including African-American and Hispanic child, is put on the American ladder of success: a good education, and a great job.

We will follow the noble example of our military men and women, working selflessly across all difference races and incomes and backgrounds, to achieve unity and accomplish amazing things.

Ladies and gentlemen of the American Legion, I ask today for the honor of your vote. Working in unison, we can deliver the real American change our country so desperately needs.

We will make America Strong Again.

We will Make America Proud Again.

We will Make America Safe Again.

We will Make America Great Again.

Thank you, and God bless.

---End of Trump Speech ---

Thank you Mr. Trump. You are the best! We are so lucky!

Before readers move on in this book, please consider going out to the web just about anywhere to hear the speech.

If you can't find any through search engines easily use this URL. https://www.youtube.com/watch?v=2ssWyu7GwtQpee

Essay 1 Jobs! Jobs! Jobs! What's the Government Doing?

Running For Congress

Hello Everybody. When I wrote this book originally in April, 2009, my name was Brian Kelly or Brian W. Kelly depending on how official you wanted to get. I was preparing to be on the ballot in the D11 PA Primary as a Democrat definitely running for Congress. I still have the same name. Here is a picture of my campaign manager and my wife plotting strategy on primary election night, 2010. My wife Pat is even more lovely in person. Note the great shirts from the campaign!

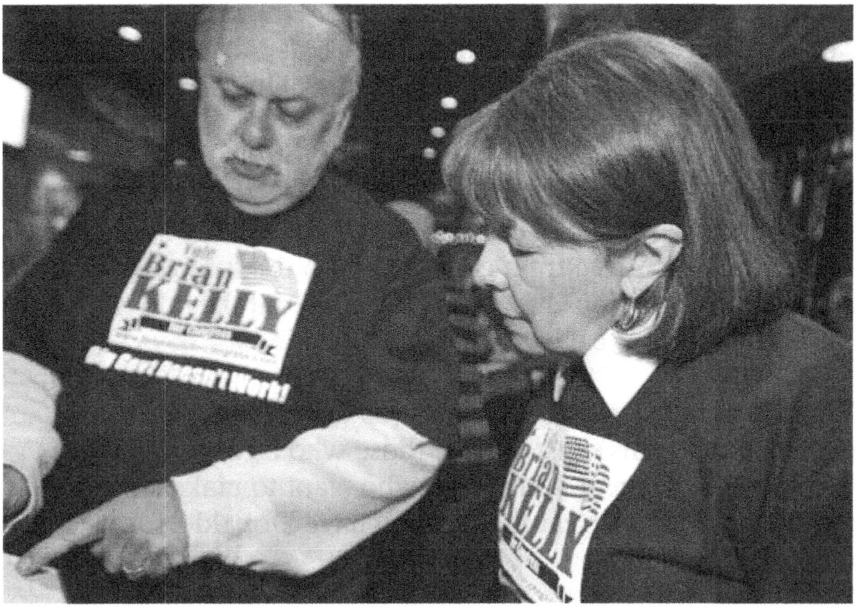

unfortunately, they have been doing so for an awful long time. They now have succeeded in making the economy so messed up that it will take years to recover. Along the way, the people of the US need Jobs! Jobs! Jobs! We need to be able to get back to work.

All the while that this "reshaping" of the US has been going on, through 2016, almost eight years into the Obama Administration, Congress and the President have been pretending that the country is already at work and that these are normal post-recession times. We are not back to work and these are not normal post-recession times.

The Democrats concentrated on their socialist agenda rather than helping Americans get back to work. Republicans wimps merely wanted to get along with the Democrats. Only once formally, that I can recall did the President say that Jobs were the most important item on his agenda.

State of the Union 2010

President Barack Hussein Obama delivered the 2010 State of the Union Address on January 27, 2010, to a joint session of Congress. It was the President's second time before a joint session of Congress. His first was a month after taking office in 2009. The President delivered the speech on the floor of the United States House of Representatives in the United States Capitol and it was aired on all major networks. Most Americans, in fear over the economic recession, anticipated that the President would offer a solution to our woes and hopefully, it would be workable, and hopefully, he would not be kidding about it.

On cue the president touched on two of the hot topics on everybody's mind. During the speech, Obama covered major proposals for Job creation and federal deficit reduction. A fly on the wall would have thought that finally the country was going to hear about a solution that would mean Jobs! Jobs! Jobs!

Looking at the President's speech, under the category of Job creation there were three major points as follows:

1. Building clean energy facilities
2. Giving rebates to Americans who make their homes more energy-efficient
3. Slash tax breaks for companies that send jobs overseas (giving those breaks to companies that create Jobs in the U.S.)

The first two items were about energy and the third was about the President being annoyed that some American corporations were not repatriating their earnings in foreign countries. In other words, the US was not getting the tax revenue. So, the only apparently meaningful thing in the president's speech on Jobs was actually about something else. Obama never cared about jobs. It's the only answer as to why!

The next point in his speech on "Jobs" was to "encourage American innovation." On the surface one could see how this could help the Jobs situation. The funny thing about the comment is that Americans have always been innovative. Look at the list of inventors and inventions of Americans from electricity to the iPad. In the write-up of the State of the Union, as a clarifying point the part about encouraging American innovation had a subtle subtitle (focus on clean energy).

Michael Moore, the well-known progressive filmmaker and liberal thinker loves using a basketball analogy to describe President Obama. Moore says that many times President Obama "fakes right and goes left." In other words, this artful speaker is often all words and no action or different action. Once he's convinced the folks that he is doing one thing, they relax and then right before their eyes he pulls the fake and goes left. He often gets away with it because nobody would expect him to be so obvious. He is the master of the unexpected. For example, most of us expected him to want to be a good president.

During the State of the Union, it was another presidential head fake. It turns out that there were few bullets of substance on jobs— mostly just lip service. His Jobs message was an energy message as the President at the time was quite desirous of having the Senate pass the Jobs killing Cap and Trade bill that had already passed the House. It is hard to be for Cap and Trade and increased Jobs! at the same time but Obama still thinks he is ambidextrous.

His second head fake was when he offered these two bones to Congress. Note again these are energy issues, not Jobs issues:

- ✓ Building nuclear power plants
- ✓ Exploring off-shore areas for oil and gas

If the President was interested in building nuclear power plants or exploring off-shore areas for oil and gas, we would have been doing this for the last eight year. But remember, he fakes right and goes left. Sorry folks, but on the Jobs thing, he was just kidding. Before we go back to the 2010 State of the Union, the defining speech of the Obama presidency, let's just see how well Mr. Obama has done on jobs.

Jobs! Jobs! Jobs! from inauguration to 2016

The President could not have liked Investor's Business Daily's report on jobs from March 2016. It brings us right up to date on success with Jobs so let's go over it now. I suspect there was too much truth in this analysis for Obama's tastes.

For example, the President has been bragging about a 14.4 million job growth number. That sounds impressive doesn't it? But the president's number is stretched over almost six full years, while other factors were changing concurrently. For example, during the same period, the working age population grew by 15.8 million. So, the normal growth to sustain jobs was not met. We were short by 1.4 million jobs. We have definitely lost ground on jobs under Obama.

Besides that, the supposed 14.4 million increase in jobs is measured against when the job market hit rock bottom in February 2010 after over a year of Obama, a big recession, and no prospects for an improved economy. If you compare the current number of jobs to the previous jobs peak two-years earlier during the Bush years, in January 2008—which, by the way is how job growth is normally measured—the number of private-sector jobs has increased by just 5.6 million.

Additionally, when we include the period from 2008 instead of beginning at 2010, during the same time, the population grew by more than 20 million. In other words, there's what can be called a "*jobs gap*" of more than 14 million. That is a lot of jobs that Obama policies kept out of America.

Let's now look at the figure that the President does not want any of us to see. What about "labor force participation"? This is a measure of how many people are working or activity looking for a job. Admittedly, it has recently ticked upward, it is still way below where it was when the jobs recession ended in early 2010.

Let's put this in context with the Reagan recovery. If we compare the Administration's numbers to what happened during the Reagan recovery, when the job market exploded after bottoming out in December 1982. While the population grew 12.4 million in the following six years, the number of jobs shot up by 18.4 million. Yes, I said "UP!"

Clean coal was just another head fake

At some point even president Obama stopped talking about clean coal, which right now is a myth perpetrated by those who think they can con the environmentalists into seeing something that is not. A year or so after Obama's 2010 SOU, on July 14, 2011, American Electric Power announced it would table plans to build a carbon capture and sequestration project at its Mountaineer Plant in West Virginia. This ended the short-term notion of clean coal for West Virginia.

Yet, coal is really big in West Virginia. And, so, West Virginia University keeps looking for new ways of doing things that can make the technology even cleaner. But nothing in technology happens overnight. It takes a lot of research, and sometimes an idea takes 20 years to develop.

"If coal is going to be here for 250 years, we're going to need newer technologies as we go into the next 250 years that would make coal more energy efficient and make it easier for us to extract these technologies in a cleaner way with less damage to the environment," said Richard Bajura, director of the National Research Center for Coal and Energy at West Virginia University. That day is not here yet but recreational basketball and head fakes to the people are a real thing for sure.

Coal is extremely energy rich and it would be good if a little soap could clean it up. A single fist-size lump of bituminous coal contains about 12,000 Btu--enough energy to power a 75-watt bulb for two days. Coal is relatively easy to dig out of the ground and it is still dirt-cheap. Coal costs about 1/6 of oil or natural gas per Btu. Like it or not, a substantial portion of the industrial world was built with coal power and coal keeps it going.

Of course coal has issues. Its ashes are not very pleasant nor is its smoke. We might call these sooty particulates. Coal also has sulfur and nitrogen compounds. These cause acid rain. And, yes, there are traces of mercury and other toxic metals in a wad of coal.

Despite the challenges of purely clean coal, coal-fired power plants are much cleaner than they once were. They are still considered bad news for the environment and human health. Despite this, it is a sure thing that in the northeast especially for many years before the natural gas revolution in the late 1960's, there would have been hundreds of thousands of deaths if there were no coal to heat homes. The question then was can death by freezing during an excessively cold and dank winter evening be a better deal than expiring from an abundance of sooty particulates over a minimally shortened lifetime.

By the way, there is no such thing as an average lifetime. My grandmom and grandpop lived well into their eighties. Gene Wilder, one of my favorite actors died this past week at 83. Gram and gramps lived in our home until they died. We had a Heatrola Stove in between the Dining Room and the Parlor and there was a Wilkes-Barre Stove in the kitchen to heat that area, cook, and provide hot water for the house. We had no furnace.

We took the ashes out and dumped them in the back yard in an area where grass refused to grow. Chicken or Egg? I would bet that my grandma and grandpa would say if asked that coal lengthened their lives. It is a matter of perspective.

The environmentalists would rather people freeze to death than have any emissions at all. It is no coincidence that many leading environmentalists are also major population control proponents. Any motivation that elevates a certain chemical composition of the atmosphere above human life is misguided at best. So, a few frozen bodies every now and then is preferable to some environmentalists than a disfigured tree a bit too close to a nearby coal chimney.

This is not a moral or immoral book though some might argue that no jobs when there can be jobs is a moral issue. Few Americans that I know would carry it as far as major elites in our society such as CNN Founder Ted Turner's perception of how to make sure the environment is clean and safe for him: " "A total population of 250-300 million people, a 95% decline from present levels, would be ideal." Why guys like Turner are not interested in more coal deaths is a mystery indeed.

A recent study concluded that coal emissions contribute to 10,000 premature deaths in the United States each year. I'd like to see that study. How do they know? Besides early deaths, they say that coal is by far the largest single source of greenhouse gases in the U.S. So it is no surprise that coal has long been the primary target of proposals to cut air pollution and carbon-dioxide emissions. One might ask with all the emissions going on in the world, especially China, how is it that anybody or anything is alive?

Just in time to skirt the various plans to cap or tax CO2, coal is getting rebranded. In my opinion, this is claptrap. The new buzzword we already discussed is "clean coal." It is a high-tech, low-emissions fuel of the future. I don't doubt coal can be made cleaner and it should but it will never be clean and clean coal is certainly not an option today. If it were, the US would become the "Saudi Arabia of clean coal overnight." By the way, we are already listed as having more gas and oil than Saudi Arabia or any other country.

One might ask: Why try to reduce our dependence on coal today when fabulous, guilt-free clean coal is just around the corner? The facts again speak loudly: Coal will never be clean. It is possible to make coal emissions cleaner and as noted previously, we should go as far as economically possible to do so. But coal as an energy source has helped my family live our lives in a warm home. It also has provided many jobs to many family members and others in Pennsylvania and other states. It sure can be called a poor man's fuel but it is a powerful energy source for our country.

Let's be clear. We should continue research into making coal cleaner--that fuel will be a vital part of our energy mix for decades. Right now it is just a good thought for the future. Meanwhile we have a lot of work to do to create real-world energy alternatives that work today. All of this work and the energy we get adds to the number of jobs available and that is a good thing.

Obama, the "Jobs Man" made just a few comebacks in eight years

On January 27, 2010 we finally got the "I am the Jobs Man Message." The news of the big nothing Jobs plan did not even have a chance to hit the next day talk shows when Nancy Pelosi could contain herself no longer. Most people had not yet gotten the Obama jobs message when, bursting with self-pride, the Madame Speaker at the time purposely puppetted an overly prepared parody of herself and Obamacare to the American people. I love alliteration.

Having listened to the State of the Union and its mention of Jobs, I originally thought that the Speaker was off message. Maybe she had not gotten the Jobs message that Obama was putting forth. Nope! She knew that it was just a head fake. She read it better than any of us. Her wait was over.

She could have rolled with it a few more days so it looked more legitimate--like it was real, but I repeat, she could not contain herself. The President had to get that darn State of the Union out of the way so he could give the head fake. Nancy Pelosi was full of glee. She caught the fake and she no longer had to wait to deliver her message, which I have word for word just below: I did add a small preamble to the Pelosi speech so it reads like the way I just described. Here it is

Where has Congress been on Jobs?

Why is it that the past four Congresses have not been interested in creating more Jobs for workers? Congress has not even had enough time for persuasive rhetoric. They are simply MIA while letting the President have his way on whatever he wants. Mr. Obama has no desire to create new jobs unless they can be government jobs.

Why is it that Congress wants to give all of the earnings of the working-person to the non-worker? There are two answers. Philosophically many Democrats have become socialists and more and more on the hard left espouse Marxism and Communism. Notice that after all Obama's head fakes, he goes left! Democrats see this as their calling. Their goal is not to create more Jobs but to create more people looking for Jobs who will be dependent on government. The President is right in tune and the Republicans have overdosed on Ambien.

That is the Democrats way of making more Americans dependent on the hand of the government and they are succeeding. When you are fortunate enough to be employed, their goals affect you differently. They want to redistribute your wages to the guy down the street who sleeps all day. The second answer is that they buy votes with your money by giving it to somebody else. This is not our parents' Democratic Party but it nonetheless is the Party as it exists today.

Healthcare Redistribution

Democrats have this notion that if you have something that somebody else would like to have that you are selfish for keeping it. So, their programs—Obama's and Hillary's programs are to take away what you have and give it to somebody else with the authority of government agencies such as the IRS.

It is no wonder that they also believe in healthcare redistribution and though nobody talks about it like this. Democrats in Congress do not want your employer to give you healthcare benefits. They know that people who are employed typically have health insurance. Often the health policies are good. They want the people who do not work to have the same health insurance policies as you do. They want the people who never put a dime into Medicare to have the same health benefits as retired seniors.

The only way for Congress and Obama to do that is to redistribute your healthcare. Since your employer is not going to pay for people who do not work for the company, and Medicare right now, will not pay for those who are not entitled to Medicare; the solution is to take half of the value of your plan and give it to somebody else. They have been doing it for most of the Obama years.

Additionally, they have taken 1/2 of Medicare (this is in the operative bill) and given it to somebody else. This is called healthcare redistribution and it means that those who earned their health insurance are being forced through taxation and insurance rates to give it up for weakened insurance policies so that in the end, all policies are the same and there is equality.

Under the program we find that there is less and less healthcare but there is more equality. Few people today have a good health insurance policy for a reasonable price. But there are now others who get subsidies so they can afford better policies than you. Is this why you sent your Congress person to represent you? Rationing, longer lines in the doctor's office and the ER as well as reduced care are the natural effects. It was a bad bill and it has been hurting a lot of people who wake up and find themselves on the outside looking in. Employers are so afraid of it, they try to reduce employee hours or reduce their workforce.

The next step towards honesty is to actually call the program "healthcare rationing." At a $trillion dollars in cost, the money is coming out of somebody's pocket. It is your pocket. Moreover, $500 billion came from reduced Medicare benefits. Additionally, as we learned from the recent insurance company exodus from Obamacare, it has already cost the insurance industry many, many billions of dollars. But, they have a choice and they are bailing!

All of these socialist programs together have been slowly bankrupting this country and destroying the prospects of jobs coming back. We cannot sustain the debt. If you spent like the government, you could not even get a credit card let alone a car loan. The Chinese hold a substantial part of our debt. In other words, the Chinese own a big hunk of America -- stuff that you think you own.

When the debt gets so high that the Chinese come collecting, get ready to speak Chinese as your primary language. Maybe they will give you a Job! And, by the way, at that point, our immigration problem is solved. I can assure you, with the Chinese in charge of America, replacing Obama's Czars with commissars, English and Spanish will both be second languages.

It actually is complicated but understandable. First, we need to face the truth: We're in bad shape. Then we need to unite--left and right, black and white, male and female, young and old--behind a simple truth. The United States of America was created to be a Republic, not a Monarchy, and not a socialist state. It's time to restore the Republic by putting a brand new Congress in office with ties to nobody but the people. Our first order of business in the new Congress must be Jobs Jobs! Jobs!

And, it goes without saying that to make sure this new Congress does not behave like the Republican Elite Establishment, we need to elect Donald J. Trump as President of the United States. He is one of the only people in the world who will watch Congress like a hawk and make sure they represent the people and not their own selfish interests.

Because Obama blew all the money on pet projects and opportunities to pay people to vote for him in term # 2, the economy, went neglected. Jobs! Jobs! Jobs! went neglected.

That's why our officials in Washington from the President on down focused on Obamacare instead of the economy? Nothing they tried had worked because they had tried nothing. The last good thing that happened in Washington regarding Jobs was that Bart Stupak announced he was turning in his keys at the end of this ride.

Honest Bart gave up his job after giving up his soul for Obamacare. Finally, the people saw at least one real job opening in the future! Even the Democrats in Stupak's district were enraged and they replaced Honest Bart with Dan Benishek, a Republican from the Upper Peninsula.

The people wondered and wondered and many who don't get it still wonder why neither Obama nor the Congress were concerned enough to be working to get the economy back on track, and to get people into jobs? The Cat in the Hat would see that as a real puzzlement. Others would say that Obama was giving America a lesson—a sort of comeuppance for its years of arrogance. Why would he be motivated to help Americans?

If I asked again--How can adding a trillion dollars to the federal budget for a new entitlement, one which siphons the good will of small businesses and large alike, along with their precious capital, be good for the economy? Obamacare was designed to postpone or kill economic recovery for you and me? It did just that.

Early on, Caterpillar, John Deere, Verizon and others were openly discussing the devastating effect of trying to battle the bad economy and Obama's schemes at the same time. This scheme, Obamacare is still costing jobs and it will cost a lot of regular people their insurance policies until it is repealed and replaced. It will be a long time coming unless of course a

Democratic miracle occurs and Hillary gets to eb Obama's third term. Then, nothing will get better.

After almost eight years, would it serve any purpose to ask if all of Obama's bad results were because the law of unintended consequences was at work or was it the real Obama plan? Is having the economy in the tank also part of the plan? If it is, it sure has been working.

The debt and deficit are at such record levels, a wise man would have to go along with Rosetta Stone's recommendation to learn a language that will help your future. They say Rosetta Stone has a pretty good course in Chinese. If future and past Obama's are equal, it is time that we all learn to speak Chinese. But we may get a break if we can keep Hillary out of the White House in 2017.

Jobs was not even on the government agenda for the last eight years. Who did they think they were kidding. Jobs is still not on the agenda. They lied about it for over a year, and affirmed their lie during the first big State of the Union address. Yet, they have done nothing but spend huge sums of money since Obama's inauguration. A lot of money spent for sure but no tangible results.

Did you see the shift from Healthcare to Jobs? It was either non-existent or imperceptible! I know I missed it also. Your elected officials have been busy doing everything but helping the economy get back on track. They have been destroying jobs by spending and creating debt while debating the takeover of energy and healthcare, beer and soda, toilet paper use, soft-drinks, and whether the Russians are good for their word on NUKES. They just don't get it!

They are TOO BUSY trying to destroy small businesses and Medicare with the healthcare takeover to actually try to create real jobs. Oh, and another election season is beginning so that

increasing the National Debt so that now it is so out of control, nobody even talks about it anymore.

The fact is that most jobs come from small businesses while the Democrats and Republicans over the last 30 years have let the big jobs go offshore. Another inconvenient fact is that the bulk of these tax increases will fall on small business owners. They have been tough on the economy that and another hunk of reasons such as business incompetence is why there are no jobs

An entry course in economics helps any college student know that less money with which to work, reduces capital and limits economic growth and hiring. No wise business person thinks about hiring more people while the cost to hire is being increased. The Republican controlled Congress has done nothing and Obama either really does not want to get it at all. Many suspected that he had a more insidious agenda in store for us. Some asked if it would be socialism. Now that we have experienced it, it is lots worse than even Jimmy Carter brought on America.

Who are the perpetrators of this particular fraud on Americans? It is the same group of bums who are the perpetrators for just about all of the hoaxes we have endured over the years. The difference this time is that we have their names. So, we can all blame nobody but Barack Obama and a complicit Congress for putting America on the Sci Fi Channel.

The artificial heart of the Obamacare monster, in full view of the public, was jumpstarted on Sunday March 21, as if it was a good thing for America. Au contraire—this is just about the worst that could have happened and the last five Congresses have been the worst the US has ever produced. Moreover, the official government comes complete with an equally ineffective and misguided President. Mattel has all the packaging notions it needs to make a hit product.

To add insult to injury, the number of federal employees earning more than $100,000 has jumped from 14% of all government workers to 25% today. In 2010, Government employees made at least 25% on the average more than comparable. Breitbart just released some newer numbers. Federal compensation averaged $119,934 in 2014, which was 78 percent higher than the private-sector average of $67,246. We pay them!

How is it that in this dire economy, politicians cannot reduce the government employee salaries by even a small percentage or reduce their ranks even a little to help us out of our tax burden. Instead their buddies keep getting raises. Even at the local levels there are no reductions. I am afraid it is because that would be against the politician's prime directive: "cause no harm to reelection chances."

Yes, nobody in government will be asked to share the pain. You can bet on that because at least at the local level, these are the votes that are assured each election and this set of voters cannot be disappointed.

Lower Wages/Fewer Jobs

The Heritage Foundation research shows that low-skilled and low-income workers have been the ones most clobbered by the weight of this huge healthcare bill. They lost their jobs first. Obamacare continues to impose tons of new taxes and "fees" on businesses and the prospects of this have been discouraging companies from hiring or continuing to employ those at the lower wage scales. Expect more and more pink slips.

The bottom line here is that Obamacare's higher taxes on all employers equates to fewer jobs and lower salaries. This is not good for working people?

Inept Administration

The reason this Obama recession, with no jobs, is more than the typical 11 months is that there is no remedy in place to fix it. Obama is not schooled in business. When nobody is working on something, chances are the something will not get done. Small businesses have been waiting for a sign from this inept administration that it is about to reduce their tax burden. And the result they get is just the opposite—Obamacare. This is a huge burden and there is little capital to reinvest after paying the tolls.

Obamacare is just one of many the axes that small businesses have been concerned might fall. From energy to immigration there are lots more axes to fall. Neither Obama nor Congress plan to help Americans other than to make them all dependent on the progressive welfare state that is being created. With Obama in charge, and with a do-nothing Republican Congress, there are no jobs and there will be no jobs. That is the Obama jobs plan as we get ready for 2017.

Government is not a facilitator in this problem. It never is a facilitator. It impedes and prevents business and industry from conducting business. Get out of the way Uncle Sam! When government prepares to punish business as they do so often for political reasons, it needs to be stopped. Yet, without the consent of the American people, the Obama faithful and the Democratic Congress for several years rammed it all down our throats. Now with the Republican elite establishment choosing never to fight Obama, the President is now Superman and does whatever he chooses.

We were on the precipice of a huge energy tax but the Congress stopped it thankfully. The huge healthcare tax has been with us for six years. Businesses have already reacted and continue to react by cutting jobs and / or farming jobs overseas. Government is not our friend and it is not the friend of US businesses. The jobs are gone and Obama is learning how to play the fiddle.

Remember these words, "this nation cannot survive on government jobs alone." Somebody has to do real work.

When somebody decides to really work on this problem, it can be solved, but not until that day comes.

Essay 3 Bringing Good Jobs Back to America!

Record unemployment

As noted in the Essay above titled. "*Where Have All the Good Jobs Gone?*" unemployment in the US for years has been at record levels. The financial collapse of 2008 started it all and it created a lull in buyer confidence and of course that resulted in significantly less sales for all companies. When sales stop, so does hiring.

If buffoons or perhaps my favorite, 435 blocks of cheap rock, or 435 well-used mop-heads had taken over Congress in 2009, they would have already done better. If there were a right way and a wrong way to get something done, the past and current Congresses in all circumstances went the wrong way despite cautions over and over from worried constituents.

When the people said, "no bailouts," Congress responded with TARP and the bailouts. When the people said "no" to the pork and the opportunities for Congress to buy votes for their 2010 to 2014 elections, at a cost over $800 Billion, Congress responded with the stimulus bill. While it was being debated, this bill was rightfully renamed by Republicans as the Porkulus bill. It is a national shame. It was supposed to be a jobs bill. If it created another job tomorrow, that new job would be lonesome.

When the people cried out for tax relief for individuals and for small businesses, Congress chose instead to continue taxing. They led with Cap and Trade in the House, more spending, more bailouts, and of course more porkulus. That was not enough. Then despite vocal opposition from Americans everywhere, Congressed rammed through the Obamacare package and the funeral bells played in the background.

Obamacare has already cost seniors and it has been taxing the country another $2 trillion over the ten years of its life at a time that there just is nothing more for Americans to give. It is a jobs killer. The taxation winds blow in many directions. Just a few years ago, the winds were brewing for a Value Added Tax rather than stop spending and become fiscally responsible.

All of this taxing and spending has drained the country of capital and there is the ongoing threat of new and more costly taxes. Businesses do not operate so they can compete with each other to see who can send the most cash to Washington. Their job is to make a profit for stockholders like my wife and I—though our holdings are small. Businesses must exercise deep caution to avoid being caught by the next dumb Washington decision.

Hiring additional workers for a great idea is out of the question in times like these. It is a matter of survival and government is clearly the enemy of the people. The Democrats would like you to believe the rich are the problem. Have you ever seen a poor man hire anybody?

You and I know that you cannot spend and spend hoping to be become rich by spending. It is not going to happen - ever. Having been whacked by the EPA and other Obama regulations, businesses are very timid about their futures and their opportunities. Now, with increased expenses for healthcare, businesses are hurting more and pulling back even more. They are not dumb.

With Obamacare taking more and more of the capital and with a dismal business outlook, many businesses are about to reduce their health insurance benefits but it is even worse than that. In many cases, companies have had to make the decision to cut

The 2010 elections did not help much though the house changed from D to R. At the same time John Boehner became a coward. We don't have to discuss that any more but it is a big part of the reason Donald Trump is today's most favorite American hero.

Obama for all his faults is very resilient. I do believe he has actually died and gone to some extraterrestrial Obama land for a brief period where he got all juiced up on battery stuff. He keeps coming back like the Energizer Bunny. They feed off the same stuff. When Obama goes down again, let him lie. Like the Energizer Bunny with multiple lives and energy to spare, do not let him get into your mind. Who knows what his next trick may be.

If American sees the tricks as tricks we have a chance but if they see the tricks as Obama having had a change of heart or that the devil made him do it, America will be hurting for a long time. Each new Republican controlled Congress gives us hope but so many ineffective leaders like Boehner and Ryan who want to protect the status quo for elite establishment Republicans simply choose to let the people down.

Yet, each new Congress is a reason for hope if and only if there are more and more replacement players. Such a Congress can then enact real jobs measures by lowering the taxes on the businesses that generate jobs. The current go-along-with-Obama strategy of increasing taxes is moving the country from recession towards a depression.

Start replacing our PA players in the general election. Pat Toomey is anti-Trump and so I am anti-Pat Toomey. Removing Toomey unless he recants his support for Clinton is a must-do. It will be good for Pennsylvania. It will be good for America. It will help us begin to give businesses hope so that tax relief and hiring is the next order of the day.

Plan 2. Implement an Americans first strategy

When I wrote the first printing of this book in 2010, this headline was there. I love America. If I heard nothing more from Donald Trump, I heard that he wants to place America and Americans first in the pecking order. I thought it was me talking. How can I not be for a guy who says what I thought I said first but I won't argue the point?

Assuming one day a full Congress can be replaced by better voters than we have today—voters who are more concerned about the health of America and all Americans than they are about whether their nephew(s) get a $10.00 per hour job in some politician-controlled school district someplace. We can do much better than that!

We have the opportunity to do some big things to create an environment that is good for business, good for workers, and good for America. The lowering of taxes and perhaps some small business incubators will give at least 8 million companies reason to look forward and therefore have reasons to increase hiring. However, different measures need to be implemented for the largest American Corporations.

Quite frankly, and this is why I am not a Republican, if it were up to me, I would insist that American Corporations take an oath of allegiance to America. If they do not we publish their names on billboards across America. This whole large company solution according to my plan begins by having America's Fortune 500 Corporations admit that they are American Corporations and that they are not global entities that merely play a little softball in America. You'll see what I mean as we expand this particular essay with Plan 3.

Plan 3. Other areas in which solutions are proposed

Check out the next set of essays as the following ideas are fleshed out and you will see there is reason for optimism. The other areas that are examined include the following:

- ✓ Offshoring -- Cost in jobs and the solution
- ✓ Illegal Immigration -- Cost in jobs and the solution
- ✓ Worker Visas, such as H-1B -- Cost in jobs and the solution
- ✓ Government Regulation -- Cost in jobs and the solution

Please join us in this book by reading the solutions proposed in each of these areas above in the next set of chapters. To say the least, they are non-standard. They are designed to work.

company. If he messed up or made any demands, they held his right to his visa, and he would be back in South Africa at the drop of a hat.

As a demonstration of how endearing this company was to the foreign worker, when he finally became a citizen, he immediately gave his notice and moved to Florida. They could not do without him. Payback is a bi----. He commanded a full executive salary while in Florida and he had a full time job there besides. Some stories work out well.

The point is that foreigners will work for substantially less wages than their American counterparts in high tech jobs. Engineers, computer techs, and many people in many other occupations want to live in America. They make lots more than from whence they came and most are placed on a track to a green card and ultimately citizenship by their corporate sponsor.

As with my friend, those on such Visas do not have a real picnic before they get citizenship. Their job is to please their masters who know their plight and they know they are ripe for abuse in the workplace. They will almost do anything not to be deported and so they do what they must to satisfy the whim of their corporate sponsors. Ironically, they are far easier to deport than an illegal for if they cross their "massa"... they are done.

One of the first spigots to get shut off when the US entered this recession eight years ago was the influx of legal foreign workers. I did not happen. Who needs 'em? But, your Congress took no action even as the unemployment rate shot up to 10%. Yes, your Congress has been complicit in the Visa programs that kill American jobs and which take advantage of the job receivers. It is only fair that whatever is left from the five last pitiful Congresses should be left jobless after this next election and perhaps somebody will pick them up for the minimum wage, or hopefully a lot less!.

In my book, Taxation Without Representation (now in its third edition and available at Amazon and Kindle), I wrote a chapter on how American Corporations exploit foreign workers as well as Americans with their special government sanctioned Visa worker programs. There are over 80 different Visa programs and the H-1B is just one program that brings in 65,000 at time each year. For a few years Congress permitted corporations to bring in over 100,000 a year. Their time limit is 6years and so at any one time there might be 600,000 high tech workers in American taking our kids (college graduates) jobs.

Congress stacks the deck against Americans . Some of our trade agreements, for example, such as the WTO, have insisted on our continuing use of the H-1B program to help foreign nationals come to America. Why does the WTO get a say? And, so some suggest that we cannot summarily stop the H-1B spigot. I say we are a sovereign nation and we are in a recession and we can dam well do what we please to help our country before we help one foreign entity.

As with most trade agreements, we were out-snookered by our "adversaries: unless we went in with a give-up strategy which is more likely. Donald Trump, a master negotiator, would love to go up against any of the buffoons that negotiated the merica-last trade agreements of which we are saddled.

I joked with my Marywood Operational Management classes that in trade talks, the US negotiators are the worst able at the table. It's like as if they could do the job, they would not be chosen. It is as if they are programmed to lose. Trump knows this but he can only say so much.

I suggest to my class that it would be far better for the US to ship in a huge block of granite or even a massive pile of feces (sorry!) and place it in the area in which the US negotiators would have been placed. The block of granite or the hunk of feces would have served America's needs far better than the losers who actually sat at the table. At least we would win every now and then. With Trump, we will win all the time.

The H-1B is a terrible loss for America's best workforce, its college graduates -- our best and brightest. It is a program that at any point in time is sapping almost 400,000 jobs from the economy. It is a travesty for American workers but especially bright students graduating from America's finest Universities.

They are unemployed while they find their potential jobs taken by foreigners on Visa programs so that corporations can save money on wages. And, yes, there are times when the new H-1B worker comes in and replaces an American making two to three times as much income. The American has the pleasure of training the foreigner prior to his or her getting fired. It's not the way it is supposed to be in America. Obama, not having lived here and learned our customs perhaps does not know this.

H1B Visas for FY 2010 & 2016

We do not have to go all the way to 2016 to begin to chart the problems. For the Fiscal Year 2010 (FY 2010), the US accepted applications for H1B visas. We were in the middle of a huge recession and we were still bringing in foreigners to take the jobs of American college graduates. I find that hard to believe. Yet, it is true. Our government has chosen not to protect America or Americans.

Further proof of the Congressional Deaf ear to the plight of recent college graduates is that they actually tried to make it worse in 2013 for this last year and this year and they are likely to try again. There was proposal in 2013 to increase H1B cap from **65,000** to 110,000 and Masters quota to increase from **20,000** to 25,000. It did not go through as of March 2015. At least, for this FY 2016 season, the quota is fixed and it will be as above and no changes.

The H1B is a nonimmigrant classification used by an alien who will be employed temporarily in a specialty occupation or as a fashion model. Too bad nobody in the US can fill the bill. This really is crap and you know it is crap and Congress is still bringing in 65,000 foreigners a year under this one of 80 Visa deals to take American jobs. Ask Matt Cartwright or your own Congressman about that! How when Americans are unemployed can we think it is OK to bring in competent workers from overseas who will work for dirt cheap wages to become citizens?.

The filing deadline for H1B visas for Fiscal Years is typically April 1. Under current law, an alien can be in H-1B status for a maximum period of six years at a time. After that time an alien must remain outside the United States for one year before another H1B petition can be approved. Certain aliens working on Defense Department projects [DOES THIS MAKE ANY DEFENSE SENSE?] may remain in H1B status for 10 years. In addition, certain aliens may obtain an extension of H1B status far beyond the 6-year maximum period. Meanwhile a fresh college graduate is unemployed.

As noted the current law limits the cap of H1Bs to 65,000 as the number of aliens who may be issued an H1B visa or otherwise be provided H1B status in a given year. There are 50 plus other Visa programs. Why is this when Americans cannot get jobs? Ask Matt Cartwright or your own dedicated and serving Congressperson. They don't get it.

BTW, because Visa holders are documented, that may be why border jumpers are called undocumented? What about the Visa holders who just never go back, and choose to just blend into the US landscape? Does documentation really matter to the unemployed American worker? At least half of illegals are visa overstayers and since nobody is asking corporations about their employees, after the visa expires, these guys still get paid but not much.

The following quote is from the first version of my book, Taxation Without Representation:

to hear. The way this program is used is a travesty. We are not talking about students. Sometimes we are talking about Professors who will work for peanuts. We are talking about workers who are in advanced areas and for the promise of a green card or the right to eventually live in America, they forego six years working for minimal wages while Americans either more so or at least equally qualified remain unemployed.

Americans expect to make a decent wage and none of us are depending on the good will of a corporate manager to decide whether we get put on a fast track to citizenship. Thankfully we are already citizens but our Congress denigrates us and denies us our natural opportunities. What a shame! What a sham!

Can we not all agree to send all 435 members of Congress and the 100 Senators home packing--most in November and the rest when their time comes--for the harm they cause American workers and visitors who should go home loving America. They have no right to stay. They agreed to go home to get the visa but they do not go home. But, why in the first place should they be granted your child's job for six years before anybody thinks about giving them the boot?

As with all the problems we identify in this book about Jobs! Jobs! Jobs!; there is an essay, aka a chapter, coming soon that offers real solutions. Your current Congress has chosen to not consider making it better. So, let's make sure they do not have the opportunity ever again. For America, we have a general election coming.

If you choose to vote for an incumbent, then you had better have the courage to ask your guy or gal what they will do under circumstances as presented in this book. If you do not get what you want from those in the finer class, boot them out. Tell everyone you know to boot them out now. I do not care if they are R or D or L or I or C or whatever, if they are not for America, their time is up! Good Bye!

Essay 5 Offshore Outsourcing Is a Jobs Killer

Outsourcing is not always offshoring

Outsourcing has been with the world for thousands of years. The sale of food, tools, and other goods from one community to another is a form of outsourcing. If you don't grow your own food then you outsource its acquisition. Outsourcing is a necessary facet of every business and it is practiced by every company because nobody can do it all. Offshore Outsourcing as practiced by American corporations, or as it is simply called, Offshoring is simply anti-American. It happens when the business believes it is so important that the workers and the country in which it is franchised, no longer matter. We can fix this!

There were US companies in the 1800s and 1900s who were vertically integrated and thus, they did it all. Rugged individualism was the credo of the day, and if you could not do it all, you could not compete. These companies took care of their own production, mining, manufacturing from raw materials, building finished goods, shipping the goods, and they sold the end products in their own stores.

Many of these companies even went so far as insuring themselves; handled their own bookkeeping and taxes; had their own lawyers etc. Some even designed and built their own buildings as it was viewed as the proper way to expand their enterprises. To do that, they required a major diversity of talent. That was then!

Eventually, in American History, it no longer was a matter of pride that a company did it all. It became very difficult to have all the talent required in one business and so companies began to concentrate on what are now called their core competencies. For example, furniture manufacturers began to get their wood from loggers rather than maintain their own forests.

Other manufacturers began to bring in raw materials that were in a more finished state from contractors -- steel sheets rather than iron ore. This is how it began. It has always been with us but it was never designed to hurt American workers. It was to give smaller manufacturers the opportunity to compete.

As service companies began to emerge, the manufacturing companies found it more productive to do business with these firms and gain a number of other services. Firms could never be the best in specific areas that were simply adjunct to their core businesses by relying only on in-house expertise. In the industrial revolution, there was a large growth in the service sector as manufacturers began to purchase needed skills. This was the first form of outsourcing.

Companies needed insurance services, architecture and engineering services, legal and accounting services, and many others. At this time in the U.S., the companies performing the outsourced work were almost always located in the U.S., and most often in the same city, just like their customers. Therefore it was not against national interests to outsource parts of the business to domestic firms.

Corporate globalization takes outsourcing offshore

As the economy became more global as fast ships and large airplanes and fast voice and data communications channels were established, this permitted people and goods and information to be moved rapidly from country to country. Because of these advances, it became feasible to move activities that were once done on-shore in the U.S. to a foreign country, off shore. This process is known as offshore outsourcing or simply as noted previously, "offshoring."

At first it was an experiment but the ingredients of success were in the cards. As relationships were formed in developing countries, it became easier and easier for the next company to do the same thing. Facilitator service companies emerged who would set up the whole offshore deal for any company that did not know how to get it done. In the beginning of course, the outsourcing channels were not greased as well as they are today.

Companies of today, who are ready to outsource, no longer have to do the work themselves. They outsource to "facilitator companies," such as IBM, to gain the outsourcing / offshoring expertise. There are many such firms that are now in place to expedite the entire process.

For the US companies that employ such offshoring avenues, it does help that they write their checks for offshoring to companies such as IBM so that it does not appear to the uninformed that they are un-American. Yet, they are un-American and IBM is un-American and it is time we call them out and show them all for what they are. I am sure you all remember the biblical saying: "If you are not with me, then you are against me."

In the last ten to twenty to perhaps even thirty years the notion of offshoring has become as commonplace as outsourcing on-shore had been. Moreover, it has gotten more and more positive press in the business community. It has become very popular, especially in large companies in which business titans and the stockholders believe their company must be as modern as the times permit. Additionally, the big consulting firms have been recommending offshoring as a solution for bad American management for many years now. The tide for years had been

taking jobs from America. Never very patriotic, this new Canadian Plant may be in North America but it is not in the United States and it took jobs from Wisconsin. This is the kind of stuff Donald Trump will stop flat.

For far too long, manufacturing trends have been characterized by an emphasis on American companies sending operations overseas in the name of cutting costs and acquiring new business in emerging markets. There was no concern that these companies were leaving Americans way behind in their wake

The American exodus began in the late 1970s and 80s, as large multinationals such as GE began offshoring production and outsourcing to foreign contractors in low-wage environments like China and Southeast Asia, paving the way for mid-market companies to do the same.

According to the top GE guy while the pillaging of the US by GE was occurring, Jack Welch, former CEO, who was a pioneer of the practice, showed no remorse. Instead of a desire to make GE more American, Welch quipped that it would have been ideal to "have every plant you own on a barge to move with currencies and changes in the economy." Thank you ~~Colin Kaepernick~~., whoops Jack Welch, for your expression of freedom in moving GE out of the USA. America appreciates your patriotism.

Indeed, GE would continue in the Welch years and with Jeffrey Immelt as CEO to send more and more of their manufacturing operations abroad. In fact, GE was so bad they pushed their parts suppliers to also make the move. Across industries, production continued its overseas migration, sparking similar moves among mid-market companies. It was the thing to do. To H_ _ _ with America!

China will take all of what America's lack of patriotism will give them. Donald Trump often speaks about the business savvy Chinese beating the US around the world because of dirty tricks. One thing is for sure. The Chinese are not just interested in building trinkets any more. The Chinese take pride in the fact that they are a big exporter and pioneers in bullet trains traveling 215 miles an hour or more. What happened to American business pride? This environmentally friendly technology has permitted China to race past the United States in the last few years.

Soon, now that the President has shut down NASA, and the US is officially out of the Space Race, China and Russia will be taking our astronauts to the space station and back. The truth is that US firms have fought so hard for profits, they have hurt the US in its ability to be a real player on the world's high tech stage.

Regarding the California rail experiment, As everyone knows, there are no high-speed trains manufactured in the United States." Thus the inflexible requirement to use US technology had been a fundamental barrier to financing high-speed rail in the US from day 1. For the past 10 years, the Chinese had patiently waited for policymakers to recognize high-speed rail in the United States as a new enterprise and that allowing trains from countries with decades of safe high-speed rail experience was needed to connect the Southwest region and start this new industry. Unfortunately, for its own reasons, the US is against rail as a national policy. I think that is stupid but more stupid would be for the Chinese to build rail in the US.

US HIGH SPEED RAIL ASSOCIATION

I have written a number of articles over the years about rail. After my research I proposed an extensive railway network for the US and offered my research and additional research into improved passenger rail and high speed rail in the US. I also wrote a book titled *Take the Train to Myrtle Beach.* Part of the message in the book is that you cannot get there from here. And, that is a chain.

There are a lot of jobs in a railroad revitalization in this country. In my book, in addition to showing why rail is a great mode of transportation across the world, I show how you can get to Myrtle Beach from anywhere in the Northeast even though you have to stop your trek in Florence SC and rent a car for the last 100 miles to Myrtle Beach. Rental car companies in the area will be happy to pick you up at the Florence Train Station.

Having an interest in passenger train service in the US, especially High Speed Rail, I am most supportive of the US High Speed Rail Association. Donald Trump is going to latch onto their work and piggy back from it to a transcontinental railroad revival—this time with high speed rail.

Their mission is to build widespread public, business, and political support for a major investment in a national high speed rail network.

USHSR is the only organization in America focusing entirely on advancing a state-of-the-art national high speed rail network across the country. They are an independent, nonprofit 501(c)(6) trade association chartered to organize and mobilize the industry with a shared vision for a 21st century, 17,000 mile national high speed rail system built in phases for completion by 2030. Though I like that…I think we can do better.

This new national electric transportation project will revive our economy and manufacturing sector by creating millions of new jobs. It will be the catalyst for the next real estate boom, significantly reduce our dependence on oil, shrink our national carbon footprint, reduce congestion, and create efficient mobility that's safe and affordable for its passengers.

Vision

Our vision includes a national HSR Express system connecting cities and states into an integrated system, laid out in phases with an aggressive schedule for full system build out. Our vision sets high standards for interoperable, state-of-the-art dedicated track, advanced control systems, elegant multi-modal train stations, and top-of-the-line 220 mph trains connecting major cities together. Our plan calls for a support network of 110 mph trains connecting smaller cities and towns together with the high speed system.

I love the idea but I also like the idea of an extremely fast high speed cross country train from Washington DC to San Francisco. The Chinese could build it for us tomorrow. Having said that, I want ti built American. But, if I were in charge, I would use the same chinese designers to put together the plan and then have Chinese monitors to assure the rail system is built as good as it can be. That means max speeds of 360 miles per hour rather than 220. It is called not reinventing the wheel. Once we build our own US expertise, we can take high speed anywhere in the country and the world. Why not?

Shanghai Maglev, also known as Shanghai Transrapid, was once the fastest train in the world. CRH 380A running between Beijing and Shanghai, was manufactured by CSR Qingdao Sifang Locomotive & Rolling Stock. AGV Italo, touted to be the most modern train in Europe. It has a maximum operational speed of 360kmph as of Aug 29, 2013. Things keep getting faster—even computers. Japan now holds the record.

The corporate income tax is jobs' bad guy

The real culprit for greedy US corporations to turn their backs on America is the corporate income tax. Just look at the balance sheets of American corporations who do lots of work overseas. These companies have figured out how to stiff the US corporate tax system by doing business in foreign countries, and keeping their profits without declaring taxes. Donald Trump knows the system and he will bring equity back to the American people from those who take advantage of us.

The jobs are not about to come back immediately for lots of good reasons. Companies make too much money to ever decide to help the home country without big change in the U.S. tax system and the way corporations and their executives are treated in the U.S. The Trump corporate tax will bring most home. The RRR plan, which we're expecting Trump will endorse shortly will bring them all home.

While the government thinks they are nailing corporations with excessively high taxes (35%), corporations have been proving that they have more might than the US government as they pack up their bags, their plant, and a few of their people, and they take a quick and permanent trip overseas—mostly to avoid the sting of American taxes.

Jobs will not come back without major change. Right now, once a company sets up shop in a foreign country, it is a sign of management failure to come back to the US. Management would always decide that 500,000 regular employees should be fired rather than one manager. It's a culture thing. Top managers protect top managers. I point that out so that we all have little sympathy for American managers who ship jobs overseas.

IBM offshoring example

Today's poster child for treating workers poorly is the IBM Corporation. IBM has fired as many as 200,000 employees and has shipped their jobs overseas in the last twenty years. Plant sites such as Endicott, New York are decimated as is Rochester Minnesota and other huge hallmarks of IBM's onetime relationship with its American host. Today IBM and even Microsoft and Apple could care less about America and Americans.

What IBM executives, such as their chairman Virginia Rometty, are doing in the US today is dumping experienced and expensive people, who work in expensive countries (US) and moving jobs to low cost countries, using the cheapest resources available there. IBM has decided that the US is an expensive country. Ask them at their next stockholders' meeting.

The IBM Company is pushing everything that can be offshored overseas as fast as it can. If the Chinese built a high speed rail over the ocean, IBM would be its first customer. Additionally, since IBM got so good at stiffing its own workers, it has made a business out of it. IBM makes a ton of money helping other "American" Corporations do the same thing. Thank you IBM!

To further explore the Offshoring dilemma and to pick up a few really good solutions to keep jobs in the US, please continue with the next essay titled: "Greed Is the Secret for Returning Jobs to America!"

Essay 6 Greed Is the Secret for Returning Jobs to America!

Greed is the true answer!

"Corporations have been enthroned and an era of corruption in high places will follow, and the money power of the country will endeavor to prolong its reign by working upon the prejudices of the people until all wealth is aggregated in a few hands and the Republic is destroyed."

Who do you think said this?

Could it be: Barack Obama? George Bush? Ronald Reagan? Sean Hannity? Keith Olberman? Katie Couric?

If not the famous, then who? Tom Stites, the author of one of my sources for this piece thinks that the inflammatory rhetoric may "sound like a protester railing against the World Trade Organization?" Then he inquires as I just did in these words:

"Think again. These are the words of a successful corporate lawyer who represented railroads before becoming president of the United States. They resonate for many people in this Era post-Enron, when huge hot-stock corporations have cooked deals with the aid of their auditors and Wall Street bankers to enrich executives at the expense of their employees and shareholders. In this era, corporate lobbyists and campaign donors often have their way despite the interests of the voters, when Federal Reserve figures show that the top 1 percent of U.S. households controls 38 percent of the nation's wealth. But these words... But these words were written in an 1864 letter, by Abraham Lincoln."

Despite the wishes of the Founders that corporations have only state charters, they now have great federal powers. In fact, I have seen some compare one of our largest corporations, Wal-Mart specifically to the British East India Company.

Think of that idea when you are having a cup of Tea while buying some Chinese trinkets next time you are in the big store. With Walmart as today's reincarnation of the corporate power of the huge English behemoths that helped create the first Tea Party, permit me to say that I don't think the Tea is any better.

The bottom line message is that corporations are not people no matter how much graft was gained by the greedy. In my first patriotic book, Taxation Without Representation, published first in 2008, revised and published again in 2010, and available in a third edition today at Amazon and Kindle, I used this next paragraph to sum up the chicanery that brought personhood to corporations:

"Using its power to divine intent -- even the intent of the Constitution, in 1889, in the Minneapolis & St. Louis Railroad Co. v. Beckwith case, the Supreme Court, in one of its worst rulings of all time, declared that a corporation is a person for both due process and equal protection under the law. Since Shakespeare's time It's been argued that 'something is rotten in the state of Denmark.' The 1889 Supreme Court decision helped begin the decay of the potential for the American dream, unless, of course, you have no flesh. And that, my dear readers is a travesty. The damage is done but it must be undone. Unless the Obama czars steal away our rights, the people still have the power, and we need to act judiciously through the Congress."

Once they got this acceptance as a *person*, corporations kept getting more rights as government gave in to their financial power. For example, personhood has weakened the government's ability to restrain its growth. In the 1970's corporations were awarded more rights. Now they are covered under the Fourth Amendment against warrantless searches. Fifth Amendment double jeopardy protection, Sixth Amendment right to trial by jury came at the same time. With government not able to constrain its power, in many ways corporations, along with government, who often collude with corporations, are out of control today.

Yes, I admit, we already know that but is serves the soul to remember that persons have flesh and blood no matter what crooks and thieves have declared them.

Watch what you say as corporations now have First Amendment guarantees of political speech, commercial speech, and the negative free speech right not to be associated with the speech of others.

Of the top 100 economies in the world, it has been documented that 53 of them are corporations. Think of the raw power. A nation-sized corporation has a huge treasury and it has a legion of lawyers if it wants to exercise its free speech rights in a shouting match with a John Q. Public exercising her or his free speech rights. Ask yourself, how will this battle turn out?

Can this possibly be a fair fight?

If you are interested in the sting and the stain of corporations today in America , there is a great treatise on the Web, free for the reading at the following URL: http://www.uuworld.org/2003/03/feature1a.html.

So, what can you expect from a scoundrel? US corporations want you to believe they are global corporations so that our government will let them alone to do their own thing -- even if it is to take all meaningful jobs from Americans and give them to foreigners. They are scoundrels for sure and the Attorney General should proceed against them to have the notion of personhood taken from them. They are not persons.

Can Obama help the corporate problem?

In a word, of course he can if he chooses to do so. But, thankfully he has little time left. I have full confidence Trump will solve this problem. Besides, I have not found many things that I like in the way President Obama solves problems. Mostly it is because he does not typically solve problems. He creates new problems from existing ones or he exacerbates them.

The President is rarely thinking about Brian the computer guy or Joe the plumber. He is thinking about Barack the ideologue in every move he makes. He'd get more done naturally if he cared about America.

President Obama made a speech in 2009 and in this speech, he was absolutely right. He was 100% correct. He had the right idea on offshoring. Yet, since then, unfortunately, he has done nothing about. This is what the President said about companies regarding offshoring.

From an Obama May 2009 speech

".... Even as most American citizens and businesses meet these responsibilities, there are others who are shirking theirs. And many are aided and abetted by a broken tax system, written by well-connected lobbyists on behalf of well-heeled interests and individuals. It's a tax code full of corporate loopholes that makes it perfectly legal for companies to avoid paying their fair share. It's a tax code that makes it all too easy for a number—a small number—of individuals and companies to abuse overseas tax havens to avoid paying any taxes at all. And it's a tax code that says you should pay lower taxes if you create a job in Bangalore, India, than if you create one in Buffalo, New York.

"Now, understand one of the strengths of our economy is the global reach of our businesses. And I want to see our companies remain the most competitive in the world. But the way to make sure that happens is not to reward our companies for moving jobs off our shores or transferring profits to overseas tax havens. This is something that I've talked about again and again during the course of the campaign."

Amen! But, from this great rhetoric, nothing has appeared. Where's the beef. The President's fine oratory reminded me of a guy on the sidelines complaining about the coach, when in fact, Obama is the coach. He is the president. Instead of rhetoric why are we eight years later looking for a solution he could have brought to us right in the beginning. I have figured him out on this one. Whenever he sounds like he cares about Americans, he is only kidding. Sounds too simple to be true but think about it. He is only kidding. He cares about a lot. America and Americans however, are not on his list.

In this context the President was referring to unpatriated retained earnings. This means that companies who made money overseas and included it on the books of their foreign subsidiaries as retained earnings are permitted to keep the money overseas and not bring it back to the US.

The idea is that they can spend the money where it was earned and invest more in that particular country to help sustain or grow their business. Obama's supposed beef and mine also is that by not declaring the income, they do not pay US taxes.

Overall it helps to have strong corporations that carry the American flag but, as the President notes, there are billions and billions of dollars that companies are playing with overseas thereby making more money by not declaring taxes.

treasury would help fund things like unemployment compensation as well as social security.

Noncitizens have non-rights. The "We the People" Corporation could then propose to a competing foreign company to come to America, build facilities, and employ Americans. The foreign company could then use the patent rights (only in the US) as once held by the expatriate citizen corporation.

So, a business that may not be a US citizen would be able to come in and buy or build a plant and begin to manufacture and sell similar products as the corporate scoundrel that intentionally left the protection of the U.S. And, American workers would get those good jobs again.

5% corporate tax & a two-tier tax system

So that the "We the People" Corporation does not get into a contentious argument with real American Corporations that have chosen to stay, I would introduce legislation that would change the corporate income tax system to two-tier. This would dis-incent corporations from moving jobs overseas and it would incent them to bring them back. It would be a huge, huge tax reduction.

The domestic corporate income tax rate would be lowered to 5% while the overseas tax rate for products built overseas would stay at 35%. This would encourage the world, including formerly American corporations to invest big-time in the U.S. The rationale for this is once the investments came, the jobs would flow back to the US so fast that people who thought they would never work again would see big jobs again in the US.

Penalize the bad US corporate citizens

My ameliorating friends and consigliore's tell me not to do this but my instincts are that this next notion is what is needed. I am concerned about the companies who have a huge part of their former American workforce overseas already in other countries while their former American workforce remains unemployed. So, in addition to a sweet incentive of a lower tax rate, I would like to add a bad guy fee for those who have abandoned US interests and sought to increase profits by discarding American workers.

In my plan, there would be a schedule to be created that would be called the jobs penalty schedule. It would work via a formula yet to be determined but I would propose that it would be similar if not identical to the following:

Based on the schedule, corporations would pay from 0 to 10% extra tax based on their domestic jobs profile. For example, let's say IBM's domestic employee base is determined to be 200,000 at its highest in the past 20 years. Let's also assume that its current base is 100,000. The job loss would be 100,000. To calculate the percentage job loss, put the job loss # over the current job #. 100,000 / 100,000 = 1.00. The job loss index factor therefore in this scenario is 1.00 or 100%

The formula would multiply the job loss index factor by 10% to get the additional tax percentage penalty for the corporation. If your company placed jobs overseas and if you fired American workers, you would pay from one to ten percent additional tax depending on the percentage of workers you displaced.

For IBM in this case, it would compute to 1 times 10% = 10%. To get IBM's full domestic tax rate, if IBM were the perpetrator (and from what all my friends in IBM say, IBM is an egregious perpetrator), it would be 10% in penalty plus 5% normal tax = 15%. Because IBM would be deemed to no longer be a good corporate US citizen, it would pay three times as much as a percentage than another company in taxes until it brought back its labor force to the US.

Now, suppose IBM brings back 40,000 employees. Their number of domestic employees would then be 140,000 and displaced would be 60,000. So. 60,000/100,000 = .6 or 6%. And, so, IBM's corporate tax rate, if they brought 40,000 workers back would be 5 + 6 = 11% instead of 15%. If IBM brought back all 100,000 jobs, its factor would be zero and its tax rate would go down to 5 + 0 = 5%, which would be the lowest rate possible. Then we in America could say to IBM, you are not only a good corporation, but a good "person."

The thought of bringing 40,000 or 100,000 more employees back to the U.S. probably is not a notion on IBM executives' minds at this time. This program does not care what is on their minds. IBM, Microsoft, HP, Apple, and lots other US corporations who like being known as US corporations do not have a right to positive press when they are hurting Americans.

Their greed hath no bounds. They want positive press for sure but more than that they would like the 30% corporate tax savings they would get under this plan. And the United States for giving that tax reduction would get millions of jobs back. Oh, and each one of the folks who get one of those jobs, they would be paying taxes for the good of America. It's win, win!

To say the same thing just a little more bluntly. Corporations are heartless. All of their motivations are based on greed. Even when they give something, they expect more back. Quid pro Quo would have little meaning if it were not for corporations. The corporate culture is based on greed. That is all corporations understand. They owe no allegiance to the citizens of the United States just like your neighbor does not owe you or any of your other neighbors a beer on a hot day even if he has the only cooler in town.

Don't sugar coat corporations because they will not look good anyway. Most corporate executives care about two things other than themselves, which is of course, their prime motivator. Self is a big deal in the corporate boardrooms of America. The other things they care about, after themselves is their family, and then they care about the corporation. Well! I suspect there are cases in which the two of those are reversed. After all important things are taken care of you have the proverbial customer and then all those who watch the company, everything else, and then come the employees.

Understanding CEO motivation is how we bring jobs back to America. If they are paying 35% tax while all the other Harvard guys or the Wharton School MBAs are getting the 5% rate, these guys will fear that they will be fired by the stockholders who also care nothing about John Q. but know that if the CEO is paying 30% more tax than needed, the CEO needs to be replaced. Remember before even one and two above are considered for a CEO, self is the prime motivator.

I love saying this because it is the truth. Corporate executives are motivated by greed. Their self-greed reflects the full greed of the officers of the corporation who would in a second sign up to sell out their fellow Americans for a bonus. Some might give up their cube mate for a pack of Cheetos or a Starbuck's Late'. Let me assure you ladies and gentlemen, IBM and all of the greediest corporations in the US would be very interested in saving 30% from their tax bill. They'd sell out their neighbors to get it. If you live next door to any of these scoundrels, you already know what I mean.

Getting back to the math summary, the corporate tax would be reduced every time the employee index was reduced until a company, such as IBM employed 200,000 again and then its rate would be 5%. Companies that begin to offshore would be likewise affected as their job loss index factor increases, their tax bill would increase.

This helps solve the problem of offshoring and with a 10% offshoring tax rate for corporations, it also helps make the US a more competitive country in which to invest. Many economists have offered the notion that the big barrier to success for corporations is that nasty 35% tax rate imposed by the US government. This solves that problem. Country corporations from all-over who have the freedom to make money for their home country will be knocking on the US jobs door to get in on the deal. There may not be a chicken in every pot, but how about a really new deal that puts a paycheck in every mailbox.

As noted, the US corporate income tax right now is 35% and the state corporate tax varies but it is safe to say it is about 10% as an average of all states. So, 45% of most corporate profits goes to the government today even before anything goes to investors. Perhaps states also can also be incented to reduce their rates to put more people back to work.

It is argued that the huge corporate income tax is not really paid by corporations anyway but by consumers. It is fully considered in product pricing. Interestingly, the full corporate income taxes are only paid by those industries who are US corporations and who conduct business within the U.S. The good guys pay and the bad guys get a break on their overseas earnings. This loophole would also be closed.

In the Kelly plan, which one day may be the underpinnings of the Trump Plan, to summarize the information above, the US corporate tax rate, which in Ireland, lowest in the world along with Lichtenstein and Cyprus, sits at 12.5%, would be reduced to 5%. Maybe one day we can make the rate zero (0%) to get even more foreign investments on US soil. Added to the 10% is a potential jobs penalty of up to 10% that can cause the tax to be as high as 15%. Whether the rate is 5 or 10%, however, this is substantially lower than 35%. The idea of the lower tax rate is so that American Corporations will choose to invest again in

Essay 7 Solving Jobs & Illegal Immigration Together!

Corporations that cannot outsource find another way

What a shame for corporate titans who saw their golfing buddies moving huge portions of their businesses offshore to reduce their labor cost. They saw their buddies being able to move their businesses offshore to take advantage of lower wages and their buds also got "less punitive" environmental conditions. They hoped they could figure out a way that they could create a labor force that was similar to those offshore but with their company staying in America. They succeeded.

They wanted all of the advantages and none of the disadvantages of offshoring for their companies. They wanted a cheap labor source and a labor force that would not complain at all about the work environment. The overriding problem of course for industries such as farming and meatpacking and even construction was that companies that require "American" workers in America cannot offshore the work to other countries. What a problem. These businesses were stuck in America and therefore had to hire American workers. Not so fast!

Suppose, for example, your company packs meat from animals raised on US land or suppose you are selling berries or vegetables grown on US land, or you are building homes in the U.S. You cannot take your enterprise offshore. It cannot work. The poor Corporate titans could not gain the benefits of offshoring unless magically the Chinese and Indian workforce, willing to work for peanuts was brought to the US.

It may not be Chinese workers or Indian workers but the workers came nonetheless, and they are still coming. The US government solved the problem of no labor arbitrage by taking no action when illegal foreign nationals en masse took American jobs. The companies still seem to be able to hire them with impunity and profits never looked so good as wage rates are as depressed as in the Robber Baron days. And, President Obama has no idea why there is a jobs problem.

Somebody is being taken advantage of and somebody else is out of a good job, but a corporate titan is now able to share in the bounty of offshoring without even moving the company. When the government took no overt action to stop the practice during the last several administrations, its non-action was enough to put a big smile on an industry mogul's unkind face.

With the government choosing not to enforce illegal immigration laws, companies thus became able to create little pockets of employment that had almost all of the "business friendly" characteristics and the big benefits of third world countries right here in the good ole USA. Yup! Because of lax government policy intended by the Republicans to give businesses who could not offshore the financial breaks they needed, life was good. Huge corporations were able to find labor arbitrage opportunities that had not been seen since the Robber Baron days, right here in America. Just as in those days, all the workers suffered and still suffer while management prospers.

Meatpacking industry is top of the list

The story of the meatpacking industry is an egregious affront against the American way. We all seem to think that all illegal immigrants pick berries or vegetables or otherwise work on a farm. This is not true. The once highly unionized labor force in the meatpacking industry for example once commanded 25% higher wages than other manufacturers. In the early days, meatpacking was an undesirable profession because it was dangerous work and because the wages were depressed.

With the union influence, meatpacking became a desired job because the wages grew to put the many employed black workers into the middle class. New legal immigrants from all countries saw meatpacking as an opportunity for high wages if they could get the jobs. Paying such good wages however soon was too good for companies like Swift and Tyson and others so they figured a way to get the wage rate back to slave level. They shut down their city operations; the built new plants in the middle of no place; and moved their operations to the country.

Their workers for the most part chose not to go with them. A huge proportion of those who lost jobs were black and because of the great wage they once had in this industry, they had lifted themselves well into the middle class. It was too good to last.

When they corporate moguls opened their new meatpacking facilities in rural areas, the plants were non-union or were about to be. The wages were about half of what they had been when the companies were all unionized. Along the way the meatpacking industry came up with a lot of tricks so that unions were never again able to take hold of the industry again. Illegal foreign nationals swarmed into these areas and took as many jobs as possible. They worked for peanuts. They became the offshoring tool and no business person worried about an illegal alien joining a union. It would be almost certain deportation.

Just like the government has begun to lie at a wholesale level, company managers and executives learned to lie so that they could keep their profit margins and they could also avoid jail time. The Immigration and Customs Enforcement (ICE)

These folks are not only concerned about Obamacare but the next step, a shamnesty, which then compounds the financial distress of Obamacare by adding 30,000,000 illegal aliens and their families to the welfare rolls and to the Obamacare rolls. These folks suggest that those on welfare should replace the farm workers who choose to go back to wherever they are from. Not a bad idea!

I forget where I got this but it sums it up pretty nicely

"... Why are we questioning if we should be accepting things that are illegal. If we bend the rules for one group or action, then we have to bend the rules for all or it would be 'selective enforcement' which in itself is illegal. I agree. Able-bodied welfare recipients should take the low-paying jobs. If they do not like them, it will serve as incentive to work toward something they would enjoying working at. Welfare was originally meant to assist people back up on their feet. It was not meant to be a source of life-time income."

Lifetime Guest Plan

The Lifetime Guest Plan (LGP) -- A long term immigration fix that puts Americans first! This is a book available on Amazon and Kindle. In order to gain their LGP status interlopers must promise not to be a burden (defined as costing taxpayers); never vote; never become a citizen; never take welfare, or they must voluntarily deport. The government will help in their deportation and in fact may offer a substantial stipend of $5,000 to $10,000 for those who agree to go and not come back without paying back their to-date burden.

Americans will not pay a dime. Iron clad identification databases and ID cards with biometrics will be issued and those without such identification will be deported immediately once the program is in full implementation. LGP must register, be vetted, and pay $100 minimum each year in person to continue in the program. The book shows all the details.

Essay 8 Red Tape Is a Jobs Killer

Try starting a small business in the US?

You will face a mountain of laws that say you are not worthy to run a business. That does not sound American to me; but it is true. Those who have skipped the skip or danced the dance will tell you that you have to compromise your ideals to get what you want from the government. Is that true?

No matter how good your idea, it will be all but impossible to gain the capital necessary if you are a reasonably unknown entrepreneur. But, if you know somebody who knows somebody who knows a Congressman, they tell me your business can get a boost big enough to get it started.

Doesn't that make the fur on the back of your neck stand up straight?

Maybe you don't even need to have a product or service to be successful, but let's not talk about Northeastern PA folklore. You know that is not how it should work and one day if we are smart we will find good people as our representatives. They will promise and deliver on their promises. They will change this paradigm of corruption but we must first identify good people (hint—not politicians) and then we must help them get elected as our representatives.

It can be!

Would it not be nice to have a system that empowers rather than punishes entrepreneurs --- small and home-based businesses? This can be brought about by encouraging the federal and state legislators and the municipalities to make it easy for all of us to do business in that state, or municipality just because we are all citizens of the US.

My state, Pennsylvania is as bad as the rest. I know I can't even get a permit for working on my own house without bringing in either a contractor or a priest who will say I am not lying. OK, I jest about the priest but it sure seems that way. Most of us feel it is this bad. The officials from what I have seen, like the idea of bringing in a contractor because they are more likely to understand envelope ethics than a priest.

It is widely accepted that even in a truly market-oriented economy, some level of regulation is necessary. Natural behaviors of economic agents will not always lead to perfect competition and market equilibrium. It would be nice that every business that is created, in turn creates situations in which consumers enjoy the highest possible level of enfranchisement and prosperity. Sir Thomas More and Henry David Thoreau would agree for sure. But business, does not bring Utopia, and government would pervert it if it were to come.

Nothing is perfect but regulations are so less than perfect there is an outhouse odor as you even approach a house of regulation. You know that when you try to start a perfectly safe business in which a reasonable prudent person would say -- Yeah!; there will be a bureaucrat at some level trying even harder to shut it down.

Yes, there are issues that we all need to be protected from but-- not being able to earn a living--is not one of these things. We do not have to be perfect and should not have to be perfect and none of the regulations on any set of books are perfect unto themselves.

Some suggest we need regulation for negative externalities (e.g. pollution), information asymmetries (such as a moral hazard

future. It helps to remember that businesses, not governments create jobs.

Ask any small business person about the persecution of government forms. Government rules at its lowest, inconsequential levels by providing forms which appear to be written by lawyers for lawyers but in fact they are written by bureaucrats to stifle individual opportunity. Why? Maybe if thy used proper English we would easily be able to tell they were incompetent?

Even with the forms as written, perhaps government interns can be used for startup businesses to get beyond the work just to get set up. But they are not there in the beginning. They come in afterwards to tell you that you messed up and then they fine you. Until all regulations can be reduced and simplified, the fresh minds of low-cost might help states and municipalities to voluntarily reduce the paperwork for new businesses to start up and to flourish. It's just one thought. Businesses really need a break today in many, many ways.

Looking for new jobs? All governments are negligent if they choose not to examine all the stifling regulations that may have seemed good when enacted but, which impact jobs negatively. Let's, at all levels of government, vow to remove all the idiocy from the books that we can. If we want to have jobs, the situation can be made much better so that the person or company who can provide jobs actually believes it is a desirable notion. We all know it can be made lots better.

Somehow the Federal government, the states, and even municipalities for years have thought that they had a mission from God to place roadblocks in front of all business activity. They were looking for conforming business activity.

Instead now there is no business activity to be regulated as they have been conformed out of business. Now that there is virtually no new business activity, maybe a few less roadblocks

and adverse selection in the insurance sector). And, oh, there are natural monopolies. Admittedly, they exist, albeit for a limited period of time. Isn't this all claptrap? Come on, give me a break!

The Heritage Foundation, a conservative high-values group, has come up with some good ideas regarding business and freedom. They suggest that when the hand of government rises beyond the 'minimal level', it begins to erode and corrode freedom.

We see freedom disappearing in many ways in this Obama land. Yet it is inconceivable that our own municipalities and states would limit their ability by limiting our ability to create businesses and to create business that benefits us all. Yet, they do. Municipalities and Cities and Counties and States that give regular humans an opportunity to flourish, rather than protect the favored, always do well. Northeastern Pennsylvania would not be cited in the former but there is no reason that in the future we cannot have our day.

Economic freedom is always the first to go. When government continues to interfere as it seems to like to do, at its many levels, and especially recently, this expansion of state power requires enforcement and therefore it requires funding. This funding of course is also extracted from the people.

So, by clamping down on business opportunity with regulations, ironically the government requires and thus demands more tribute to pay for the regulations. It is no wonder that many blame the lack of prosperity today on excessive regulation at all levels of government. Please Mr. Government, let business conduct business, and let charities handle the poor. Your intervention, Mr. Government makes business ineffective and it reduces individual and business and government's opportunity for prosperity.

When businesses are not confident that they will do well tomorrow, they ae unlikely to hire any new employees for the

may cause the level of activity to increase. Because there is no business is no reason for cities and states to throw their arms up in despair. Instead it is their obligation to make conditions right that somebody with a good idea can launch a business overnight if not sooner.

Where are the good bureaucrats when we need them?

have brought us such innovation, and so I question any person thinking we should turn to government for hardly any of our needs other than National Defense. Putting the government in charge of healthcare is like finding the worst player on the team when the championship game is tied in the bottom of the ninth, and pinch hitting the best player for the worst player on the team. You're going to lose. It's a certitude.

The 16th amendment like most things that may once have been properly enforced, has been perverted over the years, especially by this administration. Team Obama has openly declared that an individual's wealth should be redistributed merely because government is all powerful. So, they steal from the rich and give some alms to the poor, thereby making the poor dependent on the state.

In their newest trick with Obamacare, the government in trying to equalize everything between the workers and non-workers. They decided it was in their purview to redistribute healthcare. The last "person" in charge of anything should work for the government if you want things to work well.

In the redistribution schemes, the workers somehow do not like them but the non-workers do. It is good to help the poor. That's why charity is a virtue. It is not good to help make poor people out of those who otherwise would be fruitful contributors to their own lives. That destroys hope. You can have faith in that.

The notion of giving to those who should not need anything returns nothing to the people. The government really does decide too much. The income tax is used for social engineering. Government uses it as a tool to manage people's purchases via tax exemptions, credits, and deductions. Watch how much beer you drink; sugar you eat; and toilet paper you use because one of those video cameras that Uncle Sam is installing everywhere is going to tell on you one day soon.

People may ask, "How does a bureaucrat from the government know what is good or bad for you or for me?" We all know they do not know because most of them are unfortunately asleep or too inept to make a positive difference. The last person anybody would call if in need would be a person from the government.

Some Elements of Government Are Good

Since we need taxes to support the good parts of government that we the people control, the best tax is clearly a consumption tax. You have seen waitresses and waiters that treat your family well. I sure have. You and I know that they prefer to get cash, rather than have the tip on the bill. Why is that? It's because it is unreportable to the government. A consumption tax would get them and you and I—only when we spend a dime. If they spend their tip, they would then pay a tax regardless of whether you gave them cash or it was on the charge card.

So, a Fair Tax can save the money the government uses for the IRS to find the tips that these folks might hide. Though the drugs that a dealer sells may not get taxed, the drug dealer's purchases are all subject to the FAIR TAX. The IRS can be eliminated because nobody will have to find the dollars that are earned under the table. Instead the tax will occur when the hidden loot is spent.

So, a consumption / sales tax would force those operating outside the current income tax system to pay their fair share -- whether they are legal or illegal. In this way, nobody gets public services for free. Nobody! Why is that not something that we all like? Anybody with a job and those who receive money from those with a job all pay taxes. This lifts the burden from only those who work.

Opponents of the Fair Tax love the idea of socialism and social engineering. The income tax is their tool. That is why they love it so much. So, they will lie about the FAIR Tax such as telling you that it will hurt Senior Citizens on Social Security. That is another lie that government likes to tell. Has government ever lied to seniors? How about no COLA because the CPI (a.k.a. the inflation rate) is zero. Is that a joke? Seniors know that is a big and unforgiving lie perpetrated by Obama and this Congress and they are angry as hell about not getting a social security check increase because of a lie. What Bureaucrats say about the Fair Tax is another pack of lies.

We're hearing more and more about big cuts in Social Security and Medicare. Hopefully, the cuts will not affect those over 62 or anybody who is collecting already. But, if you are 54 or below, expect that the Democrats in government will be telling you that you are no longer in the real Social Security fund. Your net contributions will be set to set to zero and you will be starting over. Watch and see. Raises in Social Security may also be a thing of the past regardless of the inflation rate. The fact is the government is broke.

A consumption tax like the Fair Tax is visible and thus government will be accountable. Don't compare it to the Value Added Tax which the liars in the government may be implementing in addition to the punitive personal income tax. When you hear the bureaucrats tell you the Fair Tax is bad for you, please remember that it is one of the ways to save Social Security and Medicare as everybody will be contributing. So you don't get snookered by the myths, here are a few facts from fairtax.org to chew on so you can win the argument:

1. The FairTax ensures Social Security's soundness by funding it with a progressive, broad-based national retail sales tax, rather than the current regressive, narrow payroll tax.
2. The FairTax rebate zeros the retail taxation of necessities, up to poverty-level spending, for seniors.
3. The FairTax repeals the taxation of Social Security benefits and adjusts Social Security indexing to protect seniors.

4. The FairTax ends all record keeping and income tax filings of any kind for seniors, totally insulating them from the high costs and abusive tactics of tax preparers.
5. The FairTax does not tax used goods, giving low-income seniors choices.
6. The FairTax reduces manufacturers', services', and retailers' costs, allowing them to lower costs to seniors.
7. The FairTax delivers a tax holiday on IRAs and other tax-deferred plans.
8. The FairTax ends gift and estate taxes, along with all of the unfairness to heirs and complex planning for those who earned the money.
9. The FairTax allows seniors to sell their homes and pay no capital gains taxes.
10. The FairTax generates an economic boom, which eases future budget pressure on seniors' entitlements.
11. The FairTax lowers average remaining lifetime tax rates.
12. The FairTax ensures your grandchildren have the same opportunity you did.

There is another notion that a sales tax can be a very practical measure by which we will gradually wean ourselves off of our dependence on federal and state services. By slowly lowering the percentage of the tax over time, the size of the government overall can shrink and government services can eventually be returned back to state control where they belong or perhaps, other than those deemed extremely essential, they can be ended entirely and people can keep their own money. How can that be bad?

So that you understand the salient components of the Fair Tax Plan, I have captured from the http://www.fairtax.org/ site, some of its essence below.

What Is the Fair Tax Plan?

The Fair Tax Plan is a comprehensive proposal that replaces all federal income and payroll based taxes with an integrated approach including a progressive national retail sales tax, a prebate to ensure no American pays federal taxes on spending up to the poverty level, dollar-for-dollar federal revenue neutrality, and, through companion legislation, the repeal of the 16th Amendment.

That last notion, ladies and gentlemen means that Congress sets in motion the repeal of the 16th Amendment and with it goes the IRS.

There actually has been an act proposed called the Fair Tax Act (HR 25, S 296). It is nonpartisan legislation. It abolishes all federal personal and corporate income taxes, gift, estate, capital gains, alternative minimum, Social Security, Medicare, and self-employment taxes and replaces them with one simple, visible, federal retail sales tax administered primarily by existing state sales tax authorities.

Because the best approach would be a small corporate income tax in the 10% range and an offshoring penalty of another 10%, I am almost in full agreement with the FAIR TAX as proposed and would be happy to vote for it as is.

The 10% tax would still make the US the lowest taxed nation in the world at the corporate level and this would create major investment in the US. If the FAIR Tax as proposed is enacted, I would introduce legislation to permit a 10% tax penalty for American corporations that offshore jobs.

The Fair Tax taxes us only on what we choose to spend on new goods or services, not on what we earn. The Fair Tax is a fair, efficient, transparent, and intelligent solution to the frustration and inequity of our current tax system.

The following is from fairtaxnation.com. It discusses how easily Congress can switch to the FAIR TAX.

How does this sound for a draft of the 28th Amendment to the Constitution?

Judge Deborah's Proposed Fair Tax Amendment

Proposed Twenty-Eighth Amendment

Section 1. The sixteenth article of amendment to the Constitution of the United States is hereby repealed.

Section 2. The direct taxation of any corporation, small business, farming operation or private enterprise is hereby prohibited.

Section 3. The direct taxation of any private citizen's wages or earnings by Congress is hereby prohibited. Income taxes, payroll taxes, alternative minimum taxes, estate taxes, death taxes, gift taxes, corporate taxes and capital gains taxes are hereby abolished.

Section 4. A federal retail sales tax shall be instituted on the consumption of goods and services in the United States once, without exception, but only once.

Section 5. The Congress shall have power to enforce this article by appropriate legislation. This Amendment will take effect within ninety (90) days after passage of Fair Tax legislation by Congress.

H.R. 25: "A resolution to promote freedom, fairness, and economic opportunity by repealing the income tax and other

"The FairTax provides every American family with a rebate of the sales tax on spending up to the federal poverty level (plus an extra amount to prevent any marriage penalty). The rebate is paid monthly in advance. It allows a family of four to spend $27,380 tax free each year. The rebate for a married couple with two children is $525 per month ($6,297 annually). Therefore, no family pays federal sales tax on essential goods and services and middle-class families are effectively exempted on a large part of their annual spending.

"Funding for Social Security and Medicare benefits remains the same. The Social Security and Medicare trust funds receive the same amount of money as they do under current law. The source of the trust fund revenue is a dedicated portion of sales tax revenue instead of payroll tax revenue.

"States can elect to collect the federal sales tax on behalf of the federal government in exchange for a fee of one-quarter of one percent of gross collections. Retail businesses collecting the tax also get the same administrative fee.

"Strong taxpayer rights provisions are incorporated into the Act. The burden of persuasion in disputes is on the government. A strong, independent problem resolution office is created. Taxpayers are entitled to professional fees in disputes unless the government establishes that its position was substantially justified."

As the song ends, "Who could ask for anything more?"

So, it was a Democrat who really started the modern notion of bailing out the economy with tax policy. It is too bad the current President is not a good Historian. From the way he trashes the Constitution, one would think he does not understand what it is all about. Yet, he is supposedly a Constitutional Law Professor. Maybe he was out the day they talked about the enumerated powers.

Each of the periods following these tax cuts resulted in years of prosperity. Despite historical evidence as to how to bring real jobs to the country, through deep tax cuts, instead of reducing taxes, Barack Obama's solution is to increase our load and to spend his out way out of the recession. It is not working and it is threatening the solvency of the U.S. There is no money. There has been no money and with Obama spending, there can never be a balance in the treasury. The National Debt has risen by $7.7 trillion as we approach September 2016.

Obamacare is another $trillion dollars of spending -- good money after bad. It is also a jobs killer. Why are we not doing what JFK did right now? Is it possible that Obama is not as wise as JFK? Donald Trump's plan is a JFK plan.

Obama faux tax cuts

My wife Pat is a very smart and very astute individual. Hey, she married me, Hah! She recognized the increase in her pay at the beginning of the year 2009. What a great deal! She loved the extra bucks. There was more take home money!

Outrageously, the administration took credit so Pat, trusting at the time, was thanking Obama for a little extra in the paycheck. The Democrats took credit and claimed that they really had cut taxes. As one would expect, with the President saying he just put more money in people's pockets and when they actually got the money, they believed there had been a real tax cut. That is how sly our President (no for too long) actually is. He knew he was throwing out nonsense.

My wife believes people are trustworthy. She believed that her new pay amount was because she was paying less taxes as did most of America. And thus the lie. Obama lied. He actually lies quite a bit, Get used to it!

Instead of really reducing the income tax, as JFK had, Obama gave the impression he was going to reduce income taxes but it was chicanery at its best. The Obama Administration is known for its lies and this happened to be one that eventually caught up with him. Yet, everybody still loves him. But, that is another story.

The government bragged that it had stimulated the private economy by increasing the amount of money in every worker's paycheck. What a euphemism! There was no lie there. It was merely deceit. Most Americans who bought the new pay increase as a gift from the government could not believe the government would actually try to trick them.

The absolute dumbest Americans thought they had received something and even the smart ones, such as my wife, were convinced something good had happened. Obama knows how to hold the aces for sure. Nobody except some "mean Republicans" thought he was lying. Why would the government not deliver on a promise?

The government (Team Obama) was not about to admit the big lie. What they failed to mention was that they did not change the total amount of taxes due, nor did they ever intend to do so. They wanted to put some cash out and get credit for it in the polls but they never intended to give John Q. Public a real break. The scam was simple. They would simply not to take out as much from each pay. This means that all that money not withheld from paychecks added up to a big unpleasant surprise when the average citizen filed his or her returns this year.

Obama had eaten up your tax refund. By giving you pennies a week that were not real, he stole your refund check. There was nothing left for a tax refund. Surprise! Some businesses had corrected the Obama faux plan and had begun to grab more from the paychecks even earlier so the surprise was not so disheartening for some. For the workers, the payback was a big surprise.

There were a lot more surprises in a lot more areas for the full eight years. They are still coming. Obama has had a great knack of having both sides of its mouth engaged in conversation at the same time, saying different things simultaneously. Interestingly, both sides often get it wrong. Will we eventually prove that the wrongness is intentional? No, but we will all come to believe that it is.

What a ruse! Many tax preparers reported seeing shocked taxpayers having to come up with big checks to the government when they normally would get a nice refund. Was this a stimulus or was it a fraud? You won't be getting much more of the same but only because the president is almost in his last quarter. Thank God!

Does the government really want to take over health care -- of course not! Hah! They want to take over something more important to you -- your life. And, so far, with Obamacare being rammed at you so you could not stop it, they are winning. But not for long. Already the insurance carriers will no longer carry Obamacare. Now what?

My father hated liars and so do I. This administration also claims that thousands of jobs have been created or saved by their massive spending bills. Whose jobs? The Obama propaganda machine reports that there were lots and lots of jobs saved but nobody seems to be able to find them. Maybe they are in Finland at the Al Gore Auto Plant.

The only jobs we know for sure were created are the 160,000 government jobs including 16,000 to 17,000 additional friendly

The Chinese are the most likely to come collecting for your home and my home. If the Chinese own the country, then how can you or I own anything? So, when you and all of your children and my children lose your / my home, because the government, of which you and I are a complicit and consenting member as part of the "people of the US," has given the Chinese that right through accumulated debt, you and I have little claim to personal solvency in a bankrupt country. Your house and my house is already American collateral for the debt.

When the US goes bankrupt--- we -- we all, become bankrupt as our currency has no value and our country becomes fully owned by others. There will be no face of the government to which the Chinese will ask for payment. They will take your property, since by your government's shortsighted actions, you have mortgaged it all to them.

And, that is no lie!

Essay 12 Recovering From a Recession-- the Bottom Line for Jobs!

The road to recovery

In other essays, I discussed the problems and we discussed innovative solutions from cutting red tape to solutions for offshoring and illegal immigration and others. This essay is the bottom line on how to get the inertia rolling the other way. This essay outlines the road to recovery from this unprecedented recession to its fraudulent recovery.

We are clearly suffering under a mountain of debt and there are deficits scheduled from here to eternity. A Congress controlled by my party has permitted the deficit to skyrocket to just about $1.5 trillion in various years and the national debt has more than quadrupled to about $20 trillion. With these big numbers it is easy to get zero fatigue. Take a look at the chart on the next page in Figure 12-1 to get a picture at how the me generation has robbed the future. The number of zeroes are enormous

There are only two groups in America it seems who do not know the basic way to get the United States out of a recession. The two groups are the Legislative Branch (Congress) and the Executive Branch (the President and the Czars and the Bureaucrats). The Judicial Branch could help but they are too into their own ideology.

We have been in recessions before as we discussed in the last essay and they were almost all solved by doing two simple things. The government must stop spending and cut taxes. Then, and only then will the people be able to have money to spend more on real stuff. Though the budget has been a trillion and a half out of whack, it must be balanced or be on its way to being balanced to escape a further deepening recession. This chart is from the first printing of the book in 2010.

Figure 12-1 National Debt

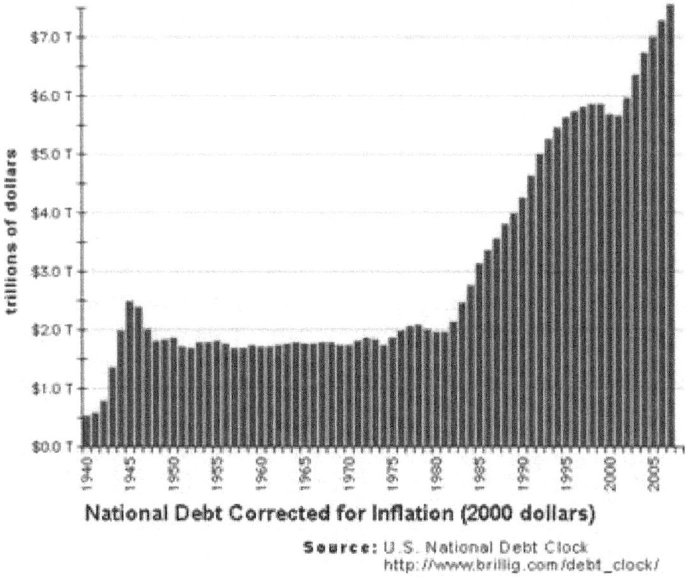

One of the dumbest things the two know-nothings (Legislative and Executive branches) considered in 2010 and might come up again is something called a value-added-tax or VAT. We must fight this with all our muscle as the fiscal end is near if a VAT is passed as it is an unseen tax and dishonest Congresses love bringing pork home unnoticed.

The VAT would not reduce the deficit anyway. In fact, it would cause the debt to continue to rise because the President and the Congress have insatiable spending appetites. They will take any money we give them to make the economy better and they will just throw it away on expanding the welfare state. This will be another tool with which the government can redistribute wealth and spend much more on stupid and frivolous projects. Maybe if they spent some money on NASA, along the way it would not be so bad but NASA is not part of the all-encompassing welfare plan. With high government spending, only the public sector benefits from the outlay. You won't get a job there but somebody who knows a politician may.

Rasmussen Polling has found the public to be well aware of how to solve the problem. Voters agree that tax cuts would help the economy lots more than increased government spending. We have seen the spending side and it does not work. The economy remains un-stimulated despite the stimulus bills and job losses continue at record paces.

Why do they not say "Enough already." Instead the Congress voted in Obamacare which at a minimum raises expenditures by $1 trillion and many are suggesting that it will eventually be more like $3 trillion.

Though interest rates are being kept artificially low, inflation is already taking hold. Please do not use the consumer price index as a guide to knowing the inflation rate as it is a formal instrument for government lying. Bureaucrats use it to dupe the public to suit their purposes.

One place it is used all the time is to set social security take home pay amounts. They lie like rugs. Go buy a rug and see if it is less expensive when the CPI is low. Better yet, go try to buy a grocery cart full of food. How is everything more expensive and yet the government tells seniors there is no inflation. Again, get its straight, they lie to suit their purposes. Vote the bums out of office.

Taxation through currency devaluation is very easy to do. Moreover it is the politically expedient course; but it is also more damaging as your dollars become the size of the one in Gordon Liddy's Rosland Capital commercial shown on page 150. Go ahead look at it now, it will crack you up!

Government cannot continue secretly taxing through borrowing (a.k.a. deficit spending) yet they are. Is the Fed secretly printing money? Inflation is socially and economically destructive in that it wipes out fortunes for those who are not invested in hard assets. If you want to know the pace at which the dollar is devaluing, look at the price of gold. The stock market is rising strangely enough but that too is because there is nothing worse to own right now than cash.

Inflation is taxation but silent. Though taxation is not the answer, if citizens were forced to pay through direct taxation up front, the voters would be shocked. They would immediately see that there really is no free lunch as promised. Though more and more people understand that nothing is free, still others think government creates money and its job is to get them their fair share.

They secretly believe that in Fort Knox and its surrounds, the US plants the whole world's supply of money trees. The dollar is the world's currency right now because these trees grow various denominations of dollars. The trees cannot grow Euros, for example. Congress would not be able to go out in public if some of the public really knew that the trees do not exist. Politicians spend the people's money. Those who think the government creates money just cannot see the problem.

Before we continue, let's review the notion of a tax. A tax simply is money collected by government directly or indirectly from the people to cover the expenditures of government.

How does the government get the people's money?

Though tax systems are supposed to be voluntary, the Government gets its money by force. We know that intrinsically. The IRS may very well be toting heat in the future when the citizens stop coughing up the cash willingly. What force is typically applied?

Government decrees that you and I and businesses will pay a percentage of our income to the Tax man (the IRS). If you or I or any business refuses, we are faced with fines, imprisonment or both. Since a business per se cannot go to jail, its officers may be held liable and they would be sent to the Big House by the IRS as necessary for it to collect what it is owed.

If somebody else took your money by threat or force, it would be stealing. Government confiscates funds and does with them as it wishes. Your dollars often wind up in the pockets of your neighbors. And, yes, it is stealing.

Let's explore this question briefly: "If government can borrow instead of tax, isn't that good for the people? It's not like the people are borrowing, right?"

Let's review how the government gets its money one more time. They take as much as is politically possible by force through the tax system using the IRS as their collectors. However, if Congress raises taxes too high, the Representatives don't get to come back to serve their next term in Washington.

So, since politicians believe that they serve because they deliver the pork to the home folks, they have figured a way to bring pork home without raising taxes. As we noted above, they know they can borrow and who cares if it is Russia or the Chinese from whom the US is borrowing. One would expect Iran not to be on the list of lenders. Again, who knows? Congress wants to be rich so bad and we pay them just under $200,000 per year.

This idea called government borrowing is a misnomer. Why the Chinese think they are going to get paid back is a mystery unto itself. There is no chance at all that the government will ever repay any of its debt. Who are they kidding? You may know that there was hardly any debt at the turn of the 20th century. It went from $2 billion to over $10 trillion in this past century, and there are at least $60 trillion in SS pension and Medicare promises via worthless IOUs that will never be paid back.

The US Congress as custodians of the treasury have served no better than a pack of charlatans. They assure their reelections by robbing the treasury to provide pork to their people. When the people take the pork, the people get the government they deserve.

Do the people get hurt when government borrows? The word again is price inflation. When government borrows, and when the Fed is operating normally instead of under Obama constraints, interest rates rise and the Fed lowers those rates by monetizing the Federal IOUs. When there is more money in circulation, your money loses its purchasing power. So, yes, the people do get hurt even when the government borrows instead of raising taxes. Government has figured out how to borrow from the invisible man. The man does not materialize but the freshly cut bills do.

If the dollar were forced to be reduced in size to match its value, Gordon Liddy would in fact have the first printed bill at the correct size for 2010 and it would be representative of bills in circulation in 2016. I love the G. Gordon Liddy Ad but do not see it enough anymore.

Whenever the Liddy Ad would come on TV, I would stop and call my wife's attention to it. It is the face of the future. If the government had to continually reduce the size of the dollar to match inflation, eventually people would need tweezers to hold on to the dollar bills once used to purchase their wares. The smaller the bill, the less it would buy. They say the penny is now worth more as a metal than its currency value. Try collecting pennies big time and watch some copper mine executives calling on you for some "ore."

If the people had to trade in their huge paper dollars for smaller and smaller sized currency worth its value, Congress's game would be up. If they taxed us, we would know it and if they had to resize the currency such as the Liddy Dollar Sizing System, to match its devaluation, we would also know it. And in all cases, G. Gordon Liddy would forever get the first reduced sized dollar. Just as the one we show below.

Figure 12-1 The Changing Size of the Dollar Bill

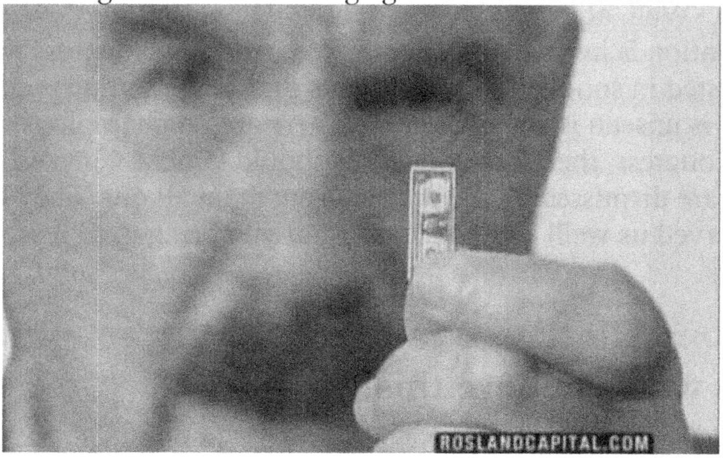

This picture above was taken in 2010 and inflation has not stopped in between then and now. Think of the dollar continually getting smaller like the Incredible Shrinking Man. Perhaps one day, even tweezers will not be small enough to pay a dollar for a dollar's worth of what once was penny candy?

Inflation without dollar resizing makes it very difficult and probably more like impossible for both consumers and businesses to plan ahead. When businesses cannot plan ahead they like to have fewer employees around to pay if they are not sure that they will need their labor.

So, Jobs! Jobs! Jobs! do not occur in times of economic uncertainty. Since this is and has been a time of uncertainty,

become a daily idea. Of course you could trust your government. After all, you elected them!

The hard-left might propose and even slicker idea. Why should you have to go to the Post Office on April 15 to fulfill a duty? The government could electronically spare you the trouble. In a perfect world, the physical dollars could be activated to flow from your wallet to the closest mailbox and they could be electronically identified as coming from you -- perhaps via a dollar / retina-like scan. Wow! Technology really can be unbelievable! Who can argue with honestly programmed technology?

Then the postman, in addition to doing regular mail, could pick up the cash from the mail box and turn it into the US treasury. It may not really be able to be done now (2016) with real dollar bills but if Obama had his way, and he could stay just a little bit longer, this could all be done electronically.

You would then have to spend only what the government has not taken. You could never cheat the government. What a great idea! Can you imagine how easy it would then be to contribute your "fair share?" Nobody would be left out of the reach of the automatic electronic hand of the IRS.

Why did nobody think of this before Obama times? Why should government be the last served? In the new system, when government needs anything, the electronic dollars, though in worth they may be the size of the Liddy Dollar bill, would be electronically lifted from your electronic wallet. You vill be happy. These dollars will then head down an electronic speedway to the electronic national treasury where you can visit them once a month but -- no touching.

The bottom line is that if every dollar spent by government came immediately out of taxpayers' wallets (your wallet), Congress might just find it impossible to fund their vast pork-barrel spending programs. You would not stand for it.

Life would become better as we would definitely throw the bums (Congress) out when the first pilferage occurred. Then, we'd all be able to plan for our future, knowing that our savings would be there and the bills would be able to be paid.

Congress gets away with this crap only because we the people accept it. Only conservatives ever line up against this and liberals, though not stupid by any means, hear our arguments but do not buy them. They'd rather pay.

The far left cannot accept that these exploding deficits mean that they are laying the burden of this huge debt pile on their children and grandchildren.

Maybe they are right! Do you think that the real hard left liberals think the next generation (grandchildren) will solve this financial dilemma? Let me ask a different way. If they felt that their grandchildren were going to be asked to pay up for grandpa's excesses, would they not stop the excesses?

Unless they think their offspring will be so smart they can figure a way out of it, or they think that money grows on trees, they can't want to dump this on the grandkids unless they are bad grand-parents.

Since they really do not want to dump all this debt (our debt) on the next generation my logic tells me that they too probably are really concerned about their kids and grandkids. Being a Democrat in today's day and age is not the answer for anybody who loves American and the idea of family and what is right!

Six years ago we should have all gotten in on the Tea Party idea. But, the mainstream media insulted all Tea-Partiers, especially Sarah Palin and the hope of conservative nationalistic populist change was muted. Instead of coming out in groups, we all waited until the next election, elected Republicans and again it did not work. So, now in 2016, the underground TEA Party is back as grandma and grandpa and we all love Donald Trump because he can recognize bull even more than a bull. Alone he has become the new TEA Party. Thank you Mr. Trump!

Back in 2010, when I first penned this book, even liberals should have been in the Tea Party. Back then, it would have been so much easier.

Today, the neighborhood liberals pretend to trust Hillary but they trust her no more than you or I. They are both embarrassed that they are called on by the mindless to love her and they are concerned that others of their ilk will mock them if they come out for Trump in any way. And so, they wait for November for a positive judgment day in which, by voting, they can tell Hillary and all the others who want to take down America to go to Hell!

Sorry if the excitement in my voice upsets anybody!

The government is all consoling and all-eradicating. Don't look for anything to be left when this administration finally gives up on socialism or it is defeated and must leave town. .

All of us have been duped into thinking it will take a long time --- why else would there be references to children and grandkids? Hah! All US citizens will be paying what can only be called a fraud tax in the months ahead as price inflation soars. It is not waiting for the grandkids to be born It is right around the corner. When it breaks loose, who are you going to blame? It won't be Ghostbusters, though we may need them for the mess!

Most will not blame the government either and that is too bad because it is all government's fault. The big culprit is the government. If the people rose up and blamed the government, we could actually solve the problem. The government is the problem. Yes, we have met the enemy and it is the government of the US. The government is the culprit, and the good news is that we have the ability and the authority to change the government. The tool we use has a simple name. It is called a "vote." Our authority comes from a document called the "Constitution."

Of all the big economic issues we face, the most serious problem is the amount the US government owes to US citizens, corporations, foreign instruments, and of course the Government Sponsored Enterprise's -- GSE (Social Security, Medicare, etc.).

This cannot be fixed with monetary policy as it will lead to hyperinflation. The losers will be those with cash or treasury bonds. The holders of such bonds could never receive fair market value for their investment. The dollars they would receive would be Liddy-sized and if China were shipped a pile of Liddy dollars in a small bag for their trillions in holdings, they might create a different kind of crisis.

I am a man looking for a solution that might even be quicker than the offshoring et al solutions explored in earlier essays. This solution would be very painful for a lot of people so even if they get a vote, the good from it will never happen. Some of this stuff has already been explored in earlier essays but let's look at it all together one more time:

Among the suggestions is to replace the income tax with the FAIR Tax. I like that an awful lot. Get rid of the Income Tax completely as we have been suggesting in prior essays. Replace it with the FAIR tax. Instead of businesses protecting their earnings by eliminating jobs, they should pay as they go and be able to plan. A consumption tax such as the FAIR tax removes the disincentive for business to invest and it creates Jobs! Jobs! Jobs! Additionally, because the tax is in the price, it has the effect of making products and services seem more expensive, and this encourages saving.

Some might call this a "virtuous cycle" as it adds to the pool of invest-able business credit; it lowers real interest rates; and it creates further business investment and jobs.

Their work helped cause the crisis and their work lengthened the recession. The CRA and poor banking regulations caused the problem. Spending money on a failed GM, on failed banks, on Freddie Mac and Fannie Mae, exacerbated the problem.

It helped keep the economy at a standstill long after it hit bottom. The people wanted no part of it. If all these deals were so good, you and I know that the three dudes in charge would have figured out some way to put some of their own sheckles into the pot to assure getting a lot of sheckles in profit returns.

The verdict on a lot of this has been in for six years, we know the bailouts and the stimulus packages all were ill conceived and doomed to failure. Only a fool would have invested in a deal that would cost more than it was worth. Barney, Chris, and Paul stuck the American people with the bill for their ill-advised largesse.

No matter what we do, GM will have cost the taxpayers $billions that will never be returned. With all the government capital, GM may have had enough good managers to keep the company from eventual real bankruptcy without more government help.

No sane person would have gone for the Frank / Dodd/ Kanjo deal. These three stooges stuck John Q. Public with the tab for their unsupportable and unprecedented schemes. For everybody but the people, the bailout decisions were good. The people will remember the members of the 2010 Congress all their lives.

Now, as if nobody remembers the truth, ironically all three of these Congressmen in 2010 lined up to take credit in their campaigns for their sheer brilliance in avoiding a catastrophe. When I look around I see something far different. In the last year of Obama, we are still living through a catastrophe. Freddie and Fannie are still bottomless pits fully subsidized by the people. Who are they kidding? The problem is not gone. Wikipedia has some good information on who Freddie and Fannie are and from whence they came:

Fannie and Freddie are bad twins!

"The Federal Home Loan Mortgage Corporation (FHLMC), known as Freddie Mac (NYSE: FRE), is a government sponsored enterprise (GSE) of the United States federal government... The FHLMC was created in 1970 to expand the secondary market for mortgages in the US."

"The Federal National Mortgage Association (FNMA), known as Fannie Mae, was set up to be a stockholder-owned corporation chartered by Congress in 1968 as a government-sponsored enterprise (GSE), [it] was set up as a stockholder-owned corporation chartered by Congress in 1968 as a government-sponsored enterprise (GSE), but founded in 1938 during the Great Depression.

Fannie and Freddie have a big role in what some might call the welfare state but it goes even further. What do these financial cousins, Fannie and Freddie actually do? Their mission was and is to buy mortgages from savings and loans, banks and other lenders. The bank makes its profit on writing the mortgage up front and Freddie and Fannie assume the mortgage. This gives more cash for banks and other lenders so they can make many more home loans.

Unfortunately for Americans, Fannie and Freddie together, right now either hold or guarantee $5.5 trillion of mortgages. This is about half of the US's outstanding home loans. Think of how big this trough can become. Thank you Barney, Chris, and Paul.

How did Freddy and Fannie go bad?

So what got these institutions in trouble? Well, as home prices fell, foreclosures went up, and lenders ran into trouble, as did Fannie and Freddie. Loans they backed went bad, capital became harder to come by and it was harder for Fannie Mae and Freddie Mac to find buyers for their loan packages. So, what did they do? The politically correct answer is that they compromised and compromised and this led to lower and lower standards and so they were "forced" to back even riskier mortgages. As we learned in 2008, all this came back to bite them. Barney, Chris, and Paul were there from the beginning, and should take credit for helping to cause the collapse.

The politically incorrect answer is that Congress repealed depression era legislation designed to prevent catastrophes such as this. Additionally, Congress passed multiple versions of the Community Reinvestment Act (CRA) -- the last update was in the Clinton years. This was so that even people without a dime could qualify to get a mortgage for a home. The main criteria was reduced to whether the potential mortgagee was breathing or not.

The CRA more or less forced banks to loan at 100%, and sometimes 105% to 110% of home value to people who could not even afford a rented apartment. The joke in states like Florida was that not only did they get a house they could not afford but there was a Lexus in the garage when they moved in -- all financed by their mortgage. While property values were rising, this was not a bad deal as everybody was a winner. As home prices fell, it all blew up in everybody's faces. Barney, Chris, and Paul were supposed to have been watching.

Barney, Chris, and Paul had the banks as well as Freddie and Fannie over a barrel so they squeezed them to take on bad loans. The system had to break. The caretakers actually broke it.

These are the kind of loans in which the mortgagee brings nothing to the closing and if need be his lawyer, at the closing, types up a fake W-2 and other needed documentation to assure the loan. Everybody at the closing and the approving bank officers all knew this was a sham.

But, by getting the documentation correct, at least the bank would have a record of why they approved the loan to the applicant. It was forced institutional fraud. Everybody knew it was a joke, but they had to commit fraud in order to be in compliance with the banking laws. In the last twenty years or so, being a liar was essential to being trustworthy in the financial industry.

There is no secret anymore. The government knows what happened. Yet, Barney, Chris and Paul are even now trying to pass legislation that makes permanent the notion of too big to fail, subtitled, the government will bail you out if you fail.

Democrats v Republicans on financial solution

In the last third of April 2010 as I was finishing this book for its first edition, the Republicans were trying to figure out how to tell the American people that the big three -- Barney, Chris, and Paul, but mostly Chris, were really not trying to regulate the industry. They were actually trying to set up the country to have to pay for the next bailout. With President Obama out on another campaign tour to sell "banking regulations" to the people, the Republican dilemma is that the people wanted good banking regulations. They could never come from Dodd-Frank!

Unfortunately, many people still trust Obama, Pelosi, and Reid, and even Paul Kanjorski, six years later for that matter. They still can't or won't believe that Congress can intentionally perpetrate a fraud on the American people. The fact is that Republicans and Democrats had a deal going to make sure the

named Donald Trump ready to take charge of the Executive Branch when elected!

To repeat, the bottom line on ending the recession is to cut spending and reduce taxes. Neither of these will occur, I am afraid, if it is left to the Obama administration. But, the good news of course is they are on their way out!

The End!

This is the formal end of this essay and the book. Thank you for being with me on this exciting journey. Remember it is up to all of us to keep our government under control and we only have one vehicle by which to do that. We must vote in all elections -- Primary and General.

While browsing the Web, I found a lot of great citizens commenting on the financial dilemma and offering their view of a good solution. All these quotes are from Sodahead.com, even if they are paraphrased. Some are so precious, the fast readers of this article (scanners) may very well skip what I wrote and go right to this good stuff. I will place any additions I made in brackets to differentiate it from all of this quoted material from "sodahead."

Ready or not, here they come, in random order

1. "And on top of that, they can get rid of all the illegal's we are supporting, cut their (the Government) wages to something more manageable by us, stop sending money to 'help' other countries when they don't do anything with the money to help themselves.

2. "Most of all I want their dang hands out of MY pockets so I have more money to spend at the store and stimulate the dang economy!

3. "Please do not discount the value of Time...we should not have to spend our Time sorting out the complexities of government tax policy. If we want to go forward, the path should be simple...we pay a fixed percentage for government services, and leave it to the elected officials to spend their "cut" to best effect.

4. "Nor will I hold my breath. The entrenched will not subscribe to change which does not benefit them.

5. "And stop sending foreign countries billions of dollars. They hate us anyway

6. "Exactly!! Sending the money we've borrowed from China to countries that steal it from the people that actually need it. Gosh.... this country is starting to sound a lot like that.

7. [This one is so good I had to find the profile of the sender. It is priceless:] [Louisa from Walkersville MD on Sodahead] "It's elementary. If you have money, you either spend it or save it. If you save it, then someone else has a chance of borrowing it thereby stimulating the economy. If you spend it then you will stimulate the economy. If you don't have money to spend or save, then you voted for Obama."

8. "I agree - The government should only be allowed to spend what it takes in taxes; and maybe the public would realize that there really is no such thing as a free lunch when they see what the real cost of all the entitlements are.

9. "It's a little like closing the barn door after the horse was stolen, but we really need a constitutional amendment to balance the budget annually.

10. "If we survive this, they will just do it again unless they are legally precluded from doing so.

12. "I agree - The federal government needs to stop all the reckless spending which would allow them to lower taxes and stop borrowing at the same time.

That's all folks

If anybody who wrote one of the above chooses to write to me, I would be happy to add your name next to your quote if you want to own up to it. The best!

LETS GO PUBLISH! Books by Brian Kelly:

(sold at www.bookhawkers.com; Amazon.com, and Kindle.).

LETS GO PUBLISH! is proud to announce that more AS/400 and Power i books are becoming available to help you inexpensively address your AS/400 and Power i education and training needs: Our general titles precede specific AS/400 and other technology books. Check out these great patriotic books which precede the tech books in the list.

The Trump Plan Solves the Student Debt Crisis
Solution for new student debt and the existing $1.3 Trillion debt accumulation

101 Secrets How to be a High Information Voter
You do not have to be a low-information voter.

Why Trump?
You Already Know... But, this book will tell you anyway

Saving America The Trump Way!
A book that tells you how President Donald Trump will help Merica dn Americans wind up on top

The US Immigration Fix
It's all in here. You won't want to put it down

I had a Dream IBM Could be #1 Again
The title is self-explanatory

Whatever Happened to the IBM AS/400?
The question is answered in this nee book.

Great Moments in Penn State Football Check out the particulars of this great book at bookhawkers.com.

Great Moments in Notre Dame Football Check out the particulars of this great book at bookhawkers.com or www.notredamebooks.com

WineDiets.Com Presents The Wine Diet Learn how to lose weight while having fun. Four specific diets and some great anecdotes fill this book with fun and the opportunity to lose weight in the process.

Wilkes-Barre, PA; Return to Glory Wilkes-Barre City's return to glory begins with dreams and ideas. Along with plans and actions, this equals leadership.

The Lifetime Guest Plan. This is a plan which if deployed today would immediately solve the problem of 60 million illegal aliens in the United States.

Geoffrey Parsons' Epoch... The Land of Fair Play Better than the original. The greatest re-mastering of the greatest book ever written on American Civics. It was built for all Americans as the best govt. design in the history of the world.

The Bill of Rights 4 Dummmies! This is the best book to learn about your rights. Be the first, to have a "Rights Fest" on your block. You will win for sure!

Sol Bloom's Epoch ...Story of the Constitution This work by Sol Bloom was written to commemorate the Sesquicentennial celebration of the Constitution. It has been remastered by Lets Go Publish! – An excellent read!

The Constitution 4 Dummmies! This is the best book to learn about the Constitution. Learn all about the fundamental laws of America.

The WebFacing Application Design & Development Guide:
Step by Step Guide to designing green screen IBM i apps for the Web. Both a systems design guide and a developers guide. Book helps you understand how to design and develop Web applications using regular RPG or COBOL programs.

The System i5 Express Web Implementer's Guide. Your one stop guide to ordering, installing, fixing, configuring, and using WebSphere Express, Apache, WebFacing, System i5 Access for Web, and HATS/LE.

Joomla! Technical Books

Best Damn Joomla Tutorial Ever
Learn Joomla! By example.

Best Damn Joomla Intranet Tutorial Ever
This book is the only book that shows you how to use Joomla on a corporate intranet.

Best Damn Joomla Template Tutorial Ever
This book teaches you step-by step how to work with templates in Joomla!

Best Damn Joomla Installation Guide Ever
Teaches you how to install Joomla! On all major platforms besides IBM i.

Best Damn Blueprint for Building Your Own Corporate Intranet.
This excellent timeless book helps you design a corporate intranet for any platform while using Joomla as its basis.
4
IBM i PHP & MySQL Installation & Operations Guide
How to install and operate Joomla! on the IBM i Platform

IBM i PHP & MySQL Programmers Guide
How to write SQL programs for IBM i